ADVANCED MODULAR MATHEMATICS

Mechanics
1

for A and AS level

The University of London modular mathematics syllabus

Graham Smithers

for

NATIONAL
EXTENSION
COLLEGE

CollinsEducational

An Imprint of HarperCollinsPublishers

Published by Collins Educational
An imprint of HarperCollins*Publishers*
77-85 Fulham Palace Road
Hammersmith
London W6 8JB

© National Extension College Trust Ltd 1994
First published 1994
Reprinted 1995, 1996

ISBN 0 00 322399 X

This book was written by Graham Smithers for the National Extension College Trust Ltd.

Designed by Derek Lee
Cover design and implementation by Derek Lee
Page layout by Mary Bishop
Project editor, Hugh Hillyard-Parker

The author and publishers thank Pat Perkins and Joan Billington for their comments on this book.

Printed and bound in the UK by Scotprint Ltd, Musselburgh

The National Extension College is an educational trust and a registered charity with a distinguished body of trustees. It is an independent, self-financing organisation.

Since it was established in 1963, NEC has pioneered the development of flexible learning for adults. NEC is actively developing innovative materials and systems for distance-learning options from basic skills and general education to degree and professional training.

For further details of NEC resources that support *Advanced Modular Mathematics*, and other NEC courses, contact NEC Customer Services:

National Extension College Trust Ltd
18 Brooklands Avenue
Cambridge CB2 2HN
Telephone 0223 316644, Fax 0223 313586

CONTENTS

MODULE

M1

Advanced Modular Mathematics

FOREWORD

This book is one of a series covering the University of London Examination and Assessment Council's modular 'A' level Mathematics syllabus. It covers all the subject material for Mechanics 1 (Module M1).

While this series of text books has been structured to match the University of London (ULEAC) syllabuses, we hope that the informal style of the text and approach to important concepts will encourage other readers, whose final examinations are from other examination Boards, to use the books for extra reading and practice.

This book is meant to be *used*: read the text, study the worked examples and work through the exercises, which will give you practice in the basic skills you need for maths at this level. As you go along, check your answers with the Solutions section. You need to cover *all* of these exercises, before moving on, because they are meant both to consolidate and to expand the examples that have preceded them. At the end of each section there is a Summary of the work that has been covered, listing the key points of that section.

There are many books for advanced mathematics, which include many more exercises: use this book to direct your studies, making use of as many other resources as you can. This book will act as a bridge between your new syllabus and the many older books that can still give even more practice in advanced mathematics.

The National Extension College has more experience of flexible learning materials than any other body (see p. ii). This series is a distillation of that experience: *Advanced Modular Mathematics* helps to put you in control of your own learning.

1

Basic skills and modelling

Certain *mathematical skills* are needed in your work throughout this module, and so this first section starts by:

● listing those particular mathematical skills that will be assumed in later sections
● looking especially at vectors, which can often provide a useful notation in mechanics.

Certain *mathematical terms* are also used in this module and therefore this section also:

● provides a glossary of these terms
● looks especially at how these terms are used in mathematical models.

Modelling is a way of describing real-life situations in terms of mathematical problems. Apart from being a useful way of approaching – and often simplifying problems – modelling often features as part of 'A' level examination questions.

Mathematical skills assumed

You should be familiar with the following:

● solving the quadratic equation $ax^2 + bx + c = 0$ by means of the formula:

$$\frac{-b \pm \sqrt{b^2 - 4ac}}{2a}$$

● solving some equations by factors, e.g.:

$$t^2 - 6t = 0 \Rightarrow t(t - 6) = 0 \Rightarrow t = 0 \text{ or } 6$$

● multiplying out brackets, e.g.:

$$(t - 1)^2 + (2t - 3)^2 = 5t^2 - 14t + 10$$

● using factors, e.g.:

$$R^2 - r^2 = (R - r)(R + r)$$

1

- the definitions and use of trigonometric functions:

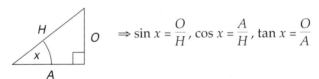

$$\Rightarrow \sin x = \frac{O}{H}, \cos x = \frac{A}{H}, \tan x = \frac{O}{A}$$

If you feel unsure about any of these topics, then a quick reference to any higher level GCSE textbook should put you right.

Mathematical skills assumed from Module P1

At various stages in the course you will also need certain topics that are covered as part of Pure Mathematics 1 (Module P1). In particular:

- Sections 5 and 8 require differentiation and integration of powers of t. For example:

$$x = 3t^2 + \frac{4}{t^2} \Rightarrow \frac{dx}{dt} = 6t - \frac{8}{t^3}$$

$$\text{and } \int \left(3t^2 + \frac{4}{t^2}\right) dt = t^3 - \frac{4}{t} + c$$

- Sections 5 and 8 require the ability to find maximum or minimum values of functions by differentiation. For example:

$$x = 5t^2 - 14t + 10 \Rightarrow \frac{dx}{dt} = 10t - 14$$

$$\Rightarrow 10t - 14 = 0 \Rightarrow t = 1.4$$

$$\Rightarrow x = 0.2, \text{ the minimum value of } x.$$

Vector notation

In Figure 1.1 you will see a grid with points A, B, C, D, E, F, G and H marked on it.

If we go from O to A, then we go 2 along the x-axis and 4 up the y-axis. We can write this as:

$$\overrightarrow{OA} = \begin{pmatrix} 2 \\ 4 \end{pmatrix}$$

Similarly we have $\overrightarrow{OB} = \begin{pmatrix} 8 \\ 2 \end{pmatrix}$ and $\overrightarrow{BH} = \begin{pmatrix} -4 \\ -5 \end{pmatrix}$

Figure 1.1

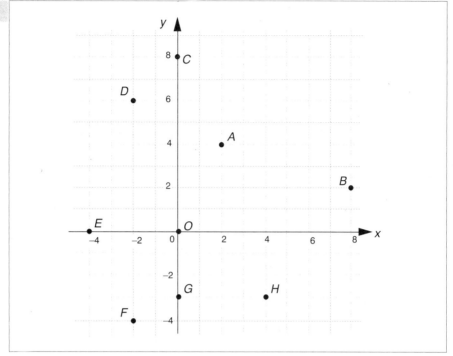

In general, if O is the origin and P has coordinates (x, y), then:

$$\overrightarrow{OP} = \begin{pmatrix} x \\ y \end{pmatrix}$$

It is conventional to call $\overrightarrow{OP}$ the position vector of P.

An alternative notation is to write:

$$\overrightarrow{OP} = x\mathbf{i} + y\mathbf{j}$$

where $\mathbf{i}$ indicates the direction of the positive x-axis and $\mathbf{j}$ the direction of the positive y-axis. In printed work, vectors are printed in bold type, as they are here; when handwriting them, we put a line underneath $\underline{i}$ and $\underline{j}$.

Example

Referring to Figure 1.1, obtain the vectors $\overrightarrow{ED}$ and $\overrightarrow{OG}$ in the form $x\mathbf{i} + y\mathbf{j}$.

Solution

$$\overrightarrow{ED} = \begin{pmatrix} 2 \\ 6 \end{pmatrix} \Rightarrow \overrightarrow{ED} = 2\mathbf{i} + 6\mathbf{j}$$

$$\overrightarrow{OG} = \begin{pmatrix} 0 \\ -3 \end{pmatrix} \Rightarrow \overrightarrow{OG} = 0\mathbf{i} - 3\mathbf{j} \Rightarrow \overrightarrow{OG} = -3\mathbf{j}$$

Example	Again referring to Figure 1.1, if $\overrightarrow{CR}$ = 4**i** – 11**j**, which of the marked points is R?

Solution	$\overrightarrow{CR} = \begin{pmatrix} 4 \\ -11 \end{pmatrix}$

∴ Beginning at C we go 4 along the x-axis and then 11 down the y-axis. But this means we finish up at H.

∴ R is the point H.

Example	A and B have coordinates (1,3) and (5,12) respectively. Write down $\overrightarrow{AB}$ and hence find AB.

Solution	A to B is 4 along the x-axis and 9 up the y-axis

$$\therefore \overrightarrow{AB} = \begin{pmatrix} 4 \\ 9 \end{pmatrix}$$

The length of $\overrightarrow{AB}$, usually called the *magnitude* of $\overrightarrow{AB}$, is written as either $| \overrightarrow{AB} |$ or, more simply, AB and can be found using Pythagoras' theorem.

$$\therefore \overrightarrow{AB} = \begin{pmatrix} 4 \\ 9 \end{pmatrix} \Rightarrow \qquad \Rightarrow | \overrightarrow{AB} | = \sqrt{4^2 + 9^2} \Rightarrow AB = \sqrt{97}$$

Example	If **a** = $\begin{pmatrix} 2 \\ 3 \end{pmatrix}$ and **b** = $\begin{pmatrix} 5 \\ -1 \end{pmatrix}$ find 3**a** + **b**.

Deduce the magnitude of 3**a** + **b**.

Solution	$3\mathbf{a} + \mathbf{b} = 3\begin{pmatrix} 2 \\ 3 \end{pmatrix} + \begin{pmatrix} 5 \\ -1 \end{pmatrix} = \begin{pmatrix} 6 \\ 9 \end{pmatrix} + \begin{pmatrix} 5 \\ -1 \end{pmatrix} = \begin{pmatrix} 11 \\ 8 \end{pmatrix}$

∴ magnitude of 3**a** + **b** (usually written as $| 3\mathbf{a} + \mathbf{b} |$) is given by:

$$| 3\mathbf{a} + \mathbf{b} | = \sqrt{11^2 + 8^2} \Rightarrow | 3\mathbf{a} + \mathbf{b} | = \sqrt{185}$$

You should now be able to answer Exercises 1 to 7 on pp. 8–9.

A glossary of mathematical terms

In your work on this module, you will meet all the following terms.

A *particle* is a body possessing some mass but with dimensions small enough for it to be regarded as a single point. (In 'A' level questions, people are usually considered to be particles.)

A *lamina* is a body which has mass and plane area but no thickness.

A *rigid body* is one in which the distance between any two of its points remains constant.

A *light rod* is a rod of negligible mass, i.e. it doesn't weigh anything.

A *uniform rod* is a rod whose mass is symmetrically distributed about its centre. And so a uniform rod of mass 20 kg (say) can be regarded as a light rod with a particle of mass 20 kg attached to its centre.

An *inextensible string* is a string which cannot be stretched.

A *smooth surface* is a surface without friction.

Mathematical modelling

When solving a problem in mechanics, factors that have a negligible effect are often ignored. This has the advantage of simplifying the problem without sacrificing too much accuracy. This 'simplified problem' is called a *mathematical model* for the real situation.

Let's illustrate this with an example: suppose we have an object suspended from a fixed point by means of a piece of string.

If it's a ball-bearing on the end of a piece of thick rope, then we would probably call the ball-bearing a *particle*.

If it's a piece of cardboard on the end of the string, then we would probably say that *a lamina* was being suspended.

If the object was an iron ball, then the weight of the string would be negligible compared to the weight of the ball. In that case we would probably say that we have a *rigid body* suspended by a *light string*.

If the object is made to slide across a table top which has hardly any roughness in it, then we would probably say that the surface was *smooth*.

Example   Anne has mass 50 kg and she is swinging on a plastic garden swing. What is a suitable model for this situation?

Figure 1.2

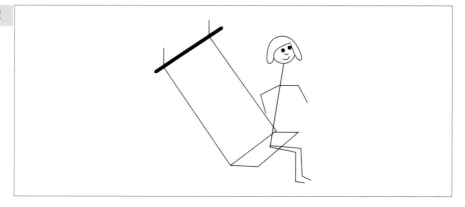

Solution   A particle of mass 50 kg suspended by a light inextensible string.

Figure 1.3

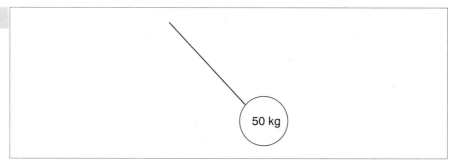

Example   Peter and John have masses 75 kg and 85 kg respectively. They are skating towards each other on an ice rink.

Figure 1.4

What is a suitable model for this situation?

Solution	Two particles of mass 75 kg and 85 kg are sliding towards each other on a smooth surface.

Figure 1.5

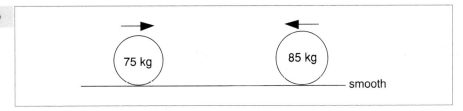

Example A 20 kg ladder leans against a wall. Julia (70 kg) is standing three-quarters of the way up the ladder.

Figure 1.6

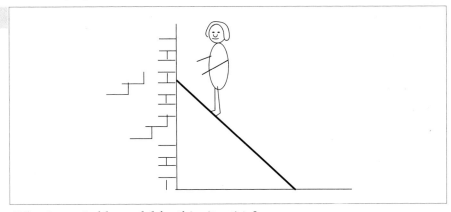

What is a suitable model for this situation?

Solution A uniform rod of mass 20 kg is leaning against a vertical wall with its foot on horizontal ground. A particle of mass 70 kg is attached three-quarters of the way up.

Figure 1.7

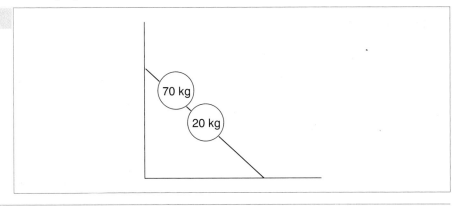

You should now be able to answer Exercise 8 on p. 9.

EXERCISES

1 Look at the grid below:

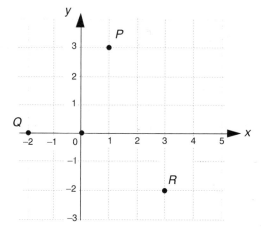

Express the following vectors in the form $x\mathbf{i} + y\mathbf{j}$

(a) $\overrightarrow{OP}$ (b) $\overrightarrow{OQ}$ (c) $\overrightarrow{OR}$ (d) $\overrightarrow{RP}$ (e) $\overrightarrow{PR}$

2 If A and B have coordinates $(2, 3)$ and $(5, 10)$ respectively, find $\overrightarrow{AB}$ and $\overrightarrow{BA}$.

3 On the grid below, mark the points A, B and C where $\overrightarrow{OA} = \begin{pmatrix} 3 \\ 2 \end{pmatrix}$, $\overrightarrow{OB} = \begin{pmatrix} 1 \\ -3 \end{pmatrix}$ and $\overrightarrow{BC} = \begin{pmatrix} 4 \\ 3 \end{pmatrix}$

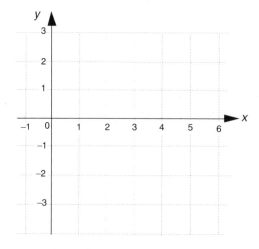

4 The position vectors of D and E are $3\mathbf{i} + 2\mathbf{j}$ and $7\mathbf{i} + 10\mathbf{j}$ respectively. Find the vector $\overrightarrow{DE}$.

5 If P and Q have coordinates $(3, 2)$ and $(5,7)$ respectively, find:

(a) $\overrightarrow{PQ}$ (b) $| \overrightarrow{PQ} |$

6 Find the distance between the points P and Q whose coordinates are $(5, -2)$ and $(7, 4)$ respectively.

7 If $\mathbf{a} = \begin{pmatrix} 1 \\ -2 \end{pmatrix}$ and $\mathbf{b} = \begin{pmatrix} 3 \\ 4 \end{pmatrix}$ find $| \mathbf{a} + \mathbf{b} |$

8 What would be suitable models for the following:

(a) a motor car
(b) a door
(c) a drinking straw
(d) a lump of coal
(e) a piece of cotton
(f) a piece of elastic
(g) a plank of wood across a stream with a man standing on it
(h) an orange
(i) a bamboo cane
(j) a cricket ball flying through the air?

SUMMARY

This section has looked at two areas that will be an important part of all the work you do in the remainder of this module:

● basic mathematical skills
● mathematical terms and how they are used in modelling.

You should now be able to:

● use vector notation, e.g.: if A has coordinates $(3,5)$ then $\overrightarrow{OA} = \begin{pmatrix} 3 \\ 5 \end{pmatrix} = 3\mathbf{i} + 5\mathbf{j}$

● work out the magnitude of a vector, e.g.: if $\mathbf{a} = \begin{pmatrix} 3 \\ 4 \end{pmatrix}$ then $| \mathbf{a} | = \sqrt{3^2 + 4^2} = 5$

● understand the meanings of terms such as particle, lamina, rigid body, light rod, uniform rod, inextensible string and smooth surface

● use the terms above to find a suitable model for a real situation.

2

Constant acceleration

We begin this section by looking at distance–time and velocity–time graphs and what we can deduce from them. This will lead on to four useful equations connecting distance, velocity and (constant) acceleration. Then, finally, we will look at a special case of constant acceleration: the acceleration due to gravity.

When you have finished this section, you should be able to:

● remember the usual units for distance, velocity and acceleration
● make deductions from distance–time and velocity–time graphs
● use the four constant acceleration equations
● tackle problems involving the acceleration due to gravity.

The units for distance and displacement

Distance is usually measured in metres. For example, a distance of 8 metres is written 8 m.

If you look at the grid in Figure 2.1, you'll see that P and Q are both 8 m from O.

Figure 2.1

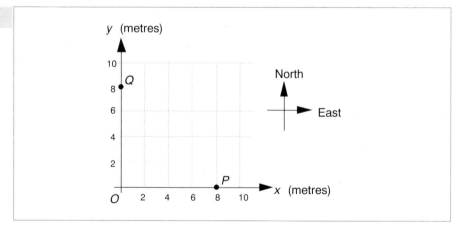

P and Q are the *same distance* from *O* but in *different places*. We say that the *displacement* of *P* from *O* is 8 m due East and the *displacement* of *Q* from *O* is 8 m due North. As you see, displacement is a distance together with a direction. In other words, displacement is a vector. And so:

Displacement of *P* from $O = \overrightarrow{OP} = 8\mathbf{i}$ (m) and *distance OP* = 8 m

Displacement of *Q* from $O = \overrightarrow{OQ} = 8\mathbf{j}$ (m) and *distance OQ* = 8 m.

The units for speed and velocity

Speed is usually measured in metres per second. For example, a speed of 12 metres per second is written 12 m/s or 12 m s^{-1}. Similarly 30 kilometres per hour may be written as either 30 km/h or 30 km h^{-1}. (Either notation is acceptable. In this module you will meet both forms of notation – this will help you become familiar with them both. In your own work you would be advised to choose the one you prefer and use that notation consistently.)

If you are driving along a straight road in a car at 20 m s^{-1}, then your speed is 20 m s^{-1}. If you then stop and start reversing at 2 m s^{-1}, then your speed becomes 2 m s^{-1}. But the directions of these speeds are different. In the first case we say that you have a velocity of +20 m s^{-1} and, in the second, a velocity of –2 m s^{-1}. And so velocity is a speed together with a direction. In other words, velocity is a vector.

The units for acceleration

Acceleration is usually measured in metres per second per second. And so an acceleration of 10 metres per second per second is written 10 m/s^2 or 10 m s^{-2}. Once again, either notation is acceptable and you need to be familiar with both of them.

Acceleration is another example of a vector. If you are gaining speed, then the acceleration is positive. If you are losing speed, then the acceleration is negative.

Distance–time graphs

Look at Figure 2.2 – what does this graph tell us? As you go from *A* to *B*, you cover 20 metres, then *B* to *C* another 20 metres and then 40 metres back to the start.

Figure 2.2

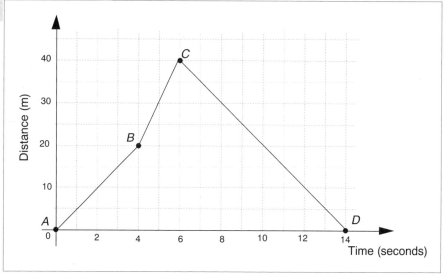

The distance from A to B is 20 m and this is covered in 4 seconds.

$\therefore$ Velocity while going from A to B is $\dfrac{20}{4} = 5$ m s^{-1}

But the gradient of AB also equals 5. And so:

> The gradient of a distance–time graph gives you the velocity.

Example   Look at Figure 2.2. Find:

(a)   the velocity while going from B to C

(b)   the velocity while going from C to D

(c)   the velocity after 10 seconds

(d)   the speed after 10 seconds

Solution   (a)   Gradient of $BC = \dfrac{20}{2} = 10$ $\therefore$ Velocity is 10 m s^{-1}

(b)   Gradient of $CD = \dfrac{-40}{8} = -5$ $\therefore$ Velocity is -5 m s^{-1}

(c)   Gradient at 10 seconds = gradient of line CD $\therefore$ Velocity is -5 m s^{-1}

(d)   Speed after 10 seconds is 5 m s^{-1}

You should now be able to answer Exercises 1 and 2 on pp. 21–22.

Velocity–time graphs

Look at Figure 2.3. What does this graph tell us?

As you go from P to Q, you get steadily faster until you reach a velocity of 10 metres per second. Then you cruise at this velocity for 2 seconds. Then, off you go again, steadily getting faster until, 4 seconds later, you reach a velocity of 20 metres per second. Finally, you gradually slow down until, after another 4 seconds, you come to a complete stop.

Figure 2.3

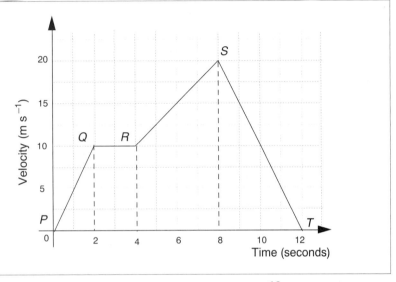

From P to Q you are getting faster. The acceleration is $\dfrac{10}{2} = 5$ m s^{-2}.

From Q to R you are going at a constant velocity of 10 m s^{-1}.

∴ You have no acceleration. And so:

> The gradient of a velocity–time graph gives you the acceleration.

But we can get more from this graph. Since you travel from Q to R at a constant velocity of 10 m s^{-1} and since this journey takes 2 seconds, *the distance from Q to R is 10 × 2 = 20 m.*

But 20 is also *the area under QR*. And so:

> The area under a velocity–time graph gives you the distance covered.

Example   Look again at Figure 2.3. Find:

(a)   the acceleration between R and S

(b)   the acceleration between S and T

(c)   the velocity after: (i) 6 seconds (ii) 11 seconds

(d)   the total distance travelled

(e)   the average speed for the whole journey

Solution
(a)   Gradient of $RS = \dfrac{10}{4}$ $\therefore$ Acceleration = 2.5 m s^{-2}

(b)   Gradient of $ST = \dfrac{-20}{4}$ $\therefore$ Acceleration = -5 m s^{-2} ($\therefore$ slowing down)

(c)   (i) 15 m s^{-1} (ii) 5 m s^{-1} Read these carefully off the graph

(d)   Look at Figure 2.4 below for the area calculations.

Figure 2.4

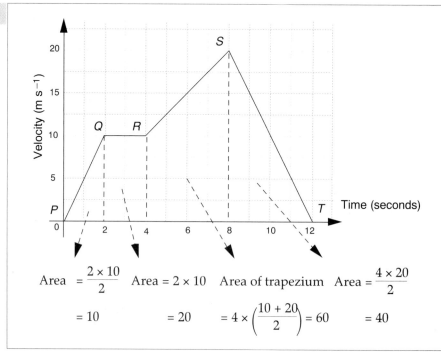

$\therefore$ Total distance covered = 10 + 20 + 60 + 40 = 130 m.

(e)   Average speed = $\dfrac{\text{Total distance}}{\text{Total time}} = \dfrac{130}{12} = 10.8$ m s^{-1} (1 d.p.)

You should now be able to answer Exercises 3–5 on pp. 22–23.

The usual symbols for displacement, velocity and acceleration

Mathematicians tend to use the same letters to represent certain things. For example, the quadratic equation is always written $ax^2 + bx + c = 0$. Very rarely do you see $\alpha f^2 + \beta f + \psi = 0$! Likewise in mechanics, certain letters stand for certain things. Let me list them for you:

s = displacement

t = time taken to cover that distance

u = initial velocity

v = final velocity

a = acceleration.

Generalising your earlier work

As we have just seen, the gradient of the velocity–time graph gives us the acceleration. Using this, together with the letters above, we get:

Figure 2.5

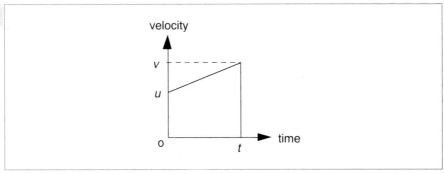

And since it's a straight line graph, we get a *constant* acceleration.

$\therefore$ Gradient $= a = \dfrac{v - u}{t}$

$\Rightarrow at = v - u \Rightarrow v = u + at$ ①

But we have also seen that the area under the *velocity–time* graph gives us the distance covered.

$\therefore$ Area $= s = t\left(\dfrac{u + v}{2}\right) \Rightarrow s = \left(\dfrac{u + v}{2}\right)t$ ②

Both equation ① and equation ② are very important. You will meet them constantly in your work on this module.

15

Example

Use the equations: $v = u + at$ and $s = \left(\dfrac{u + v}{2}\right) t$ to *deduce* the following:

1 $v^2 = u^2 + 2as$

2 $s = ut + \dfrac{1}{2} at^2$

Solution

1 Equate the value of t from the given two equations:

$$\therefore \quad \frac{v - u}{a} = \frac{2s}{u + v} \quad \Rightarrow (v - u)(v + u) = 2as \Rightarrow v^2 - u^2 = 2as$$

$$\Rightarrow v^2 = u^2 + 2as$$

2 Substitute $v = u + at$ into the equation $s = \left(\dfrac{u + v}{2}\right) t$

$$\therefore s = \left(\frac{u + u + at}{2}\right) t \quad \Rightarrow s = \left(\frac{2u + at}{2}\right) t$$

$$\Rightarrow s = ut + \frac{1}{2} at^2$$

Four constant acceleration equations

To sum up these results, you need to know and be able to use the following four equations:

$$v = u + at$$

$$s = \left(\frac{u + v}{2}\right) t$$

$$v^2 = u^2 + 2as$$

$$s = ut + \frac{1}{2} at^2$$

Let's look at some practical examples.

Example

A car accelerating uniformly in a straight line has speeds of 9 m s⁻¹ and 24 m s⁻¹ at times separated by 10 seconds. How far does it go during the period, and what is its acceleration?

Solution

Uniform acceleration $\Rightarrow$ constant acceleration

$\therefore$ We can use our four constant acceleration equations.

Let's begin by setting out the question systematically:

u	v	a	s	t
9	24	?	?	10

(We have been given u, v and t and have to find a and s.)

$\therefore s = \left(\dfrac{u + v}{2}\right)t \Rightarrow s = \left(\dfrac{9 + 24}{2}\right)10 \Rightarrow s = 165$ $\therefore$ Distance covered = 165 m

So now we have:

u	v	a	s	t
9	24	?	165	10

$\therefore v = u + at \Rightarrow 24 = 9 + 10a \Rightarrow 15 = 10a \Rightarrow a = 1.5$ $\therefore$ Acceleration is 1.5 m s⁻²

(We didn't use $s = 165$ this time, but it is always helpful if the table of results contains as much information as possible.)

Example

A train running at 16 m s⁻¹ is brought to rest with constant retardation in $2\frac{1}{2}$ minutes. How far does it travel during this time and what is its retardation?

Solution

Constant retardation means that it is slowing down at a constant rate.
$\therefore$ We can use our four constant acceleration equations.

$\therefore$
u	v	a	s	t
16	0	?	?	150

(Change the $2\frac{1}{2}$ minutes to seconds first of all)

$\therefore s = \left(\dfrac{u + v}{2}\right)t \Rightarrow s = \left(\dfrac{16 + 0}{2}\right)150 \Rightarrow s = 1200$

$\therefore$ Distance covered = 1200 m or 1.2 km

$\therefore$
u	v	a	s	t
16	0	?	1200	150

$\therefore v = u + at \Rightarrow 0 = 16 + 150a \Rightarrow -16 = 150a \Rightarrow a = -\dfrac{8}{75}$.

It is slowing down, and so the acceleration is negative.

The retardation is said to be $+\dfrac{8}{75}$ m s⁻².

Example	A skier increases her speed from 6 m s⁻¹ to 18 m s⁻¹ in a distance of 36 m. Find her acceleration.

Solution	

$$\begin{array}{ccccc} u & v & a & s & t \\ 6 & 18 & ? & 36 & \end{array}$$

$\therefore v^2 = u^2 + 2as \Rightarrow 18^2 = 6^2 + 72a \Rightarrow 288 = 72a \Rightarrow a = 4$

$\therefore$ Acceleration = 4 m s⁻²

Example	A stone is dropped down a well and gains speed at 9.8 m s⁻² . It hits the bottom 3 seconds later. How deep is the well?

Solution	

$$\begin{array}{ccccc} u & v & a & s & t \\ 0 & & 9.8 & ? & 3 \end{array}$$

(It is dropped $\therefore u = 0$.)

$\therefore s = ut + \frac{1}{2}at^2 \Rightarrow s = 0 + 4.9 \times 9 \Rightarrow s = 44.1$ $\therefore$ The well is 44.1 m deep.

Example	A cyclist starts at 1 m s⁻¹ and has an acceleration of 0.4 m s⁻² for the first 100 m of his ride. How long does he take to travel this distance?

Solution	

$$\begin{array}{ccccc} u & v & a & s & t \\ 1 & & 0.4 & 100 & ? \end{array}$$

$\therefore s = ut + \frac{1}{2}at^2 \Rightarrow 100 = t + 0.2t^2 \Rightarrow 0.2t^2 + t - 100 = 0.$

And so now we have a quadratic equation to solve!

Using the formula $\dfrac{-b \pm \sqrt{b^2 - 4ac}}{2a}$ we get:

$$t = \frac{-1 \pm \sqrt{1 + 80}}{0.4} \Rightarrow t = 20 \text{ or } -25$$

But we need a positive time $\therefore$ time taken is 20 seconds

Example	Convert a speed of 18 km/h to m/s.

Solution	18 km/hr = 18000 metres in 3600 seconds

$$= \frac{18000}{3600} \text{ m/s} = 5 \text{ m/s}$$

In mechanics, you'll often have to convert km/hr to m/s. I find it very helpful to remember this conversion rule, i.e. 18 km/hr = 5 m/s

You should now be able to answer Exercises 6 to 14 on p. 24.

Acceleration due to gravity

If you drop a stone over a cliff's edge, it will get faster and faster as it approaches the sea. This acceleration is caused by gravity. It is usually denoted by the letter g and, as far as your examination is concerned, is taken to be 9.8 m s^{-2}.

$$\therefore \text{ Acceleration due to gravity} = g = 9.8 \text{ m s}^{-2}.$$

In fact the acceleration due to gravity varies very slightly depending upon where you are. At the North Pole it is approximately 9.832 m s^{-2} whereas at Greenwich it is approximately 9.812 m s^{-2}. Then again, as you leave the earth's surface, the acceleration due to gravity decreases very slightly.

In taking g to be 9.8 m s^{-2}, what we are doing is making a mathematical model of the real situation. Since g varies only very slightly, taking it as having a constant value of 9.8 m s^{-2} will not affect significantly the validity of our results.

Example   A marble falls off a shelf 1.5 m high. How long will it take to fall?

Solution

$\downarrow$:	u	v	a	s	t
	0		9.8	1.5	?

(Falls off $\therefore u = 0$. I've added the arrow $\downarrow$ to indicate the direction of flight. You should find this helpful.)

$$\therefore \quad s = ut + \frac{1}{2}at^2 \Rightarrow 1.5 = 4.9t^2 \Rightarrow t = \sqrt{\frac{1.5}{4.9}} = 0.55 \text{ (2 d.p.)}$$

$\therefore$ The marble will take 0.55 seconds to fall.

Example   An airgun pellet is fired vertically upwards at 49 m s^{-1}.
How high does it rise?

Solution	↑:	u	v	a	s	t
		49	0	−9.8		?

(It is travelling upwards so acceleration due to gravity is negative, i.e. −9.8 m s⁻², wait)

(It is travelling upwards so acceleration due to gravity is negative, i.e. -9.8 m s^{-2}; it reaches its highest point when $v = 0$.)

$$\therefore \quad v^2 = u^2 + 2as \Rightarrow 0 = 49^2 - 19.6s \Rightarrow s = \frac{49^2}{19.6} = 122.5$$

∴ The pellet rises 122.5 m

Example   A ball is thrown vertically upwards at 8 m s⁻¹ and caught at the same height. For how long is it in the air?

Solution   First find the time to reach the highest point.

	↑:	u	v	a	s	t
		8	0	−9.8		?

$$\therefore \quad v = u + at \Rightarrow 0 = 8 - 9.8t \Rightarrow t = \frac{8}{9.8} = 0.816 \text{ (3 d.p.)}$$

The trick now is to say that *the time going up must equal the time coming down.*

∴ Total time = 2 × 0.816 = 1.63 seconds (2 d.p.)

And, incidentally, the speed with which it is caught again will be the same when it is coming down as its initial speed. ∴ It is caught at 8 m s⁻¹.

Remember these tricks – they are useful!

Example   A stone is catapulted vertically upwards at 29 m s⁻¹. For how long does its height exceed 34 m?

Solution   First find its time to reach 34 m.

∴	↑:	u	v	a	s	t
		29		−9.8	34	?

$$\therefore \quad s = ut + \frac{1}{2}at^2 \Rightarrow 34 = 29t - 4.9t^2 \Rightarrow 4.9t^2 - 29t + 34 = 0$$

Solve the quadratic and get $t = 1.16$ or 4.31.

But what can these *two* positive answers actually *mean*? The 1.61 seconds must be the time taken to reach a height of 34 m, and common sense says that the 4.31 seconds must be the time to fly up to its highest point and then back down to a height of 34 m.

∴   The time the stone is above 34 m = 4.31 − 1.61 = 2.7 seconds

Always be on the look out for these clever methods in mechanics – they save a lot of time!

Example	In the previous example, a stone was catapulted vertically upwards. What was the mathematical model? Write down some assumptions that were made.
Solutions	We modelled the stone as a particle.
	We assumed that the acceleration due to gravity remained constant and that there was no air resistance.

You should now be able to answer Exercises 15–20 on p. 24.

Practice questions

When you feel confident about the topics covered in this section, work through Exercises 21–28 on pp. 25–26. They will give you a chance to revise the work covered so far and also include questions of the sort you are likely to meet in your 'A' level examination.

EXERCISES

1 Look at Figure 2.6. Find:

(a) the velocity during the first 2 seconds

(b) the velocity after 5 seconds

(c) the velocity after 7 seconds.

Figure 2.6

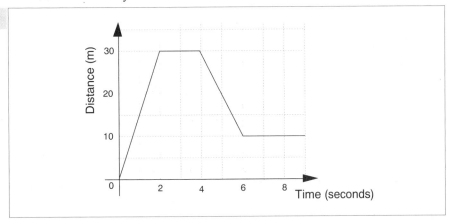

2   Look at Figure 2.7. This graph shows the distance of a train from London in km. Find the speed of the train in km h^{-1} at:

   (a)   9:05 am   (b)   9:15 am

Figure 2.7

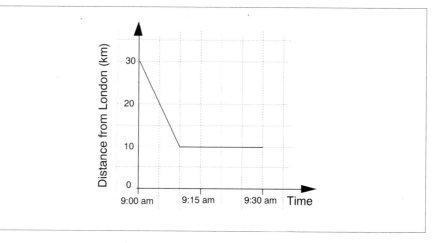

3   Look at Figure 2.8. The graph shows the velocity of a car.

   (a)   What is the acceleration for the first 4 seconds?

   (b)   What happens when $t = 4$?

   (c)   For how long is the car moving?

   (d)   For how long is the car braking?

   (e)   What is the total distance travelled?

Figure 2.8

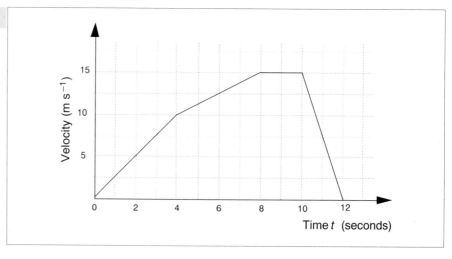

4 Figure 2.9 shows the velocity–time graph of a car journey between two sets of traffic lights.

(a) What is the acceleration of the car?

(b) What is the de-acceleration of the car?

(c) For how long does the car accelerate?

(d) How many metres does the car travel while braking?

(e) Find the distance between the two sets of lights.

Figure 2.9

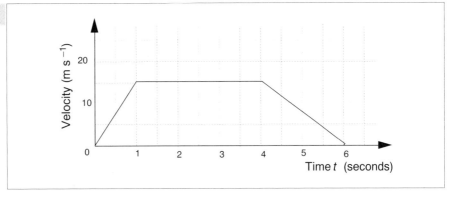

5 Figure 2.10 shows the velocity–time graph of a cross-country runner who covers three sections of the course in succession. The first is a downhill sweep, then there is a level section followed by a hill climb. Find:

(a) the acceleration of the runner on the downhill section

(b) the constant speed over the level section

(c) the de-acceleration of the runner during the hill climb

(d) the distance covered on the level section

(e) the distance covered on the hill climb

Figure 2.10

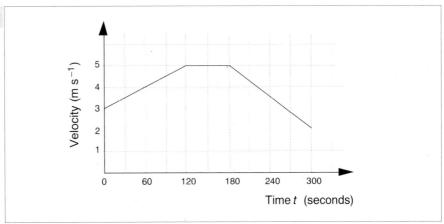

6   If a car is running along a straight road at 36 km h^{-1} and is stopped in 60 m, find the time taken to stop it.

7   If a train running at 48 km h^{-1} is stopped in 4 minutes, find the distance travelled before it is stopped.

8   A stone falling with an acceleration of 9.8 m s^{-2} starts from rest. Find its speed when it has travelled 40 m.

9   A car travelling with uniform acceleration clocks speeds of 7 m s^{-1} and 13 m s^{-1} at an interval of 3 seconds Find its acceleration.

10   A train accelerating at 0.1 m s^{-2} passes a signal box at 60 km h^{-1}. How far did it travel in the previous minute?

11   A coach travelling at 45 km h^{-1} pulls up in 100 m. What is the retardation in m s^{-2}?

12   The brakes of a train are able to produce a retardation of 1.5 m s^{-2}. In order to stop at the station, how far away must the driver apply the brakes if the train is travelling at 108 km h^{-1}? If the brakes are applied 27 m too late, with what speed will the train pass through the station?

13   A car accelerates uniformly in top gear from 14 m s^{-1} to 34 m s^{-1} in 20 seconds. Find how far it travels while accelerating, and how long it takes to cover the first half of that distance.

14   (Skill required!) A cyclist reaches the top of a hill moving at 2 m s^{-1}, and accelerates uniformly so that, in the sixth second after reaching the top, he goes 13 m. Find his speed at the end of the sixth second.

15   A stone dropped from a bridge reaches the ground in 2 seconds. How high is the bridge?

16   A cricket ball thrown vertically upwards takes 5 seconds to reach the ground again. How high does it rise?

17   A balloon which is stationary starts to rise with an acceleration of 2 m s^{-2}. What is its velocity 10 seconds later?

If ballast is dropped at the end of 10 seconds, what will be the velocity of the ballast after another 10 seconds?

18   A fire hose delivers water vertically upwards with a velocity of 20 m s^{-1}. How high does the jet reach?

19   A ball is dropped from a height of 5 m on to a stone floor. If it rebounds with half the speed with which it hits the floor, find the height to which it rises after the rebound.

20   An aeroplane diving has an acceleration of 2*g*. What additional velocity does it acquire in 10 seconds?

21 A stone is dropped from the top of a cliff. A second later another stone is thrown downwards from the same point at 11 m s^{-1}. The two stones land at the same time. Find the height of the cliff.

22 A 100 m sprinter starts with a speed 6 m s^{-1}, accelerates uniformly to 10 m s^{-1} and finishes the race at this speed. Illustrate this information with a velocity–time graph.

If her total time is 10.4 seconds, find her uniform acceleration and after what distance she is going at full speed.

23 A car takes 2 minutes to travel between two sets of traffic lights 2145 m apart. It has uniform acceleration for 30 seconds, then uniform velocity, and uniform retardation for the last 15 seconds. Illustrate this information with a velocity–time graph and hence find the maximum velocity and its acceleration.

24 A particle is initially moving at 2 m s^{-1}. Firstly it accelerates at 5 m s^{-2} for 3 seconds. Then it travels at a constant speed for the next 5 seconds. Finally it de-accelerates at 2 m s^{-2} until it slows down to a speed of 1 m s^{-1}.

Illustrate this information with a velocity–time graph and hence find:

(a)   the constant speed in the middle section

(b)   the total distance covered.

25 A particle moving in a straight line with speed u m s^{-1} is retarded uniformly for 16 seconds so that its speed is reduced to $\frac{1}{4}u$ m s^{-1}.

It travels at this reduced constant speed for a further 16 seconds. The particle is then brought to rest by applying a constant retardation for a further 8 seconds. Draw a speed–time graph and hence, or otherwise:

(a)   express both retardations in terms of u

(b)   show that the total distance travelled over the two periods of retardation is 11 u m,

(c)   find u given that the total distance travelled in the 40 seconds in which the speed is reduced from u m s^{-1} to zero is 45 m.

26 A particle A starts from the origin O with velocity u m s^{-1} and moves along the positive x-axis with constant acceleration f m s^{-2}, where $u > 0, f > 0$. Ten seconds later, another particle B starts from O with velocity u m s^{-1} and moves along the positive x-axis with acceleration $2f$ m s^{-2}. Find the time that elapses between the start of A's motion and the instant when B has the same velocity as A, and show that A will then have travelled twice as far as B.

27 Two particles P and Q move in the positive direction on the x-axis, P with constant acceleration 2 m s^{-2} and Q with constant acceleration of 1 m s^{-2}. At time $t = 0$, P is projected from the origin O with speed

1 m s^{-1}, and at time $t = 4$, Q is projected from O with speed 16 m s^{-1}. Find the times between which Q is ahead of P. Find also the distance from O at which Q overtakes P, and the distance from O at which P overtakes Q.

28 A car starts from rest at time $t = 0$ seconds and moves with a uniform acceleration of magnitude 2.3 m s^{-2} along a straight horizontal road. After t seconds, when its speed is v m s^{-1}, it immediately stops accelerating and maintains this steady speed until it hits a brick wall when it comes instantly to rest. The car has then travelled a distance of 776.25 m in 30 seconds.

(a) Sketch a velocity–time graph to illustrate this information

(b) Write down an expression for v in terms of t

(c) Show that $t^2 - 60t + 675 = 0$

SUMMARY

In this section you have investigated what is meant by distance, displacement, speed, velocity and acceleration. You started by looking at distance–time and velocity–time graphs, and then moved on to apply the four constant acceleration equations listed below. To summarise what you have achieved, you should now know that:

- the gradient of a distance–time graph gives you the velocity
- the gradient of a velocity–time graph gives you the acceleration
- the area under a velocity–time graph gives you the distance covered
- uniform acceleration means constant acceleration
- retardation means negative acceleration.

You should be able to:
- use the four constant acceleration equations:

$$v = u + at \qquad s = \left(\frac{u + v}{2}\right)t \qquad v^2 = u^2 + 2as \qquad s = ut + \frac{1}{2}at^2$$

- quote from memory or be able to work out the identity 18 km h^{-1} = 5 m s^{-2}.

You should also be able to use the following tricks in projectile questions:
- time to go up equals time to come back down
- initial speed going up equals the final speed coming down.

You should also know that, in all of these questions:
- bodies are assumed to be particles
- the acceleration due to gravity is assumed to be a constant 9.8 m s^{-2}.

3

Motion under a force

In the last section you looked at the basic principles of acceleration, and used the four constant acceleration equations to solve a number of problems. We will develop this theme in this section, by looking at the connection between force and acceleration.

When you have finished this section, you should be able to:

● distinguish between mass and weight
● work out the acceleration, given the force
● work out the force, given the acceleration
● solve problems involving connected particles.

Mass and weight

My dog has a mass of about 12 kg but, if he were on the moon, he would weigh much less – in fact he would just be floating around.

However, bring him back down to earth and all is well. His weight keeps him on the ground.

So his weight depends on gravity and the rule is:

Weight = mass × acceleration due to gravity

or $W = mg$, using standard symbols.

We saw in Section 2 that $g = 9.8$ m s^{-2}

∴ Weight of my dog = $12 \times 9.8 = 117.6$ newtons or 117.6 N

Example A brick has mass 1.5 kg. What is its weight?

Solution Weight = $1.5 \times 9.8 = 14.7$ N

(Weight is always measured in newtons, provided that the mass is in kg.)

Force

Weight is an example of a force and so all forces are measured in newtons. The force necessary to push a bag of sugar along a table top would be something like 4 N. On the other hand, if you wanted to haul a load of bricks up on to some scaffolding, the force necessary might be in the region of 500 N.

Force and acceleration: the connection

Arminder and Bobby each have a trolley to push along a long, smoothly polished hospital corridor. Bobby's trolley is twice as loaded as Arminder's.

Figure 3.1

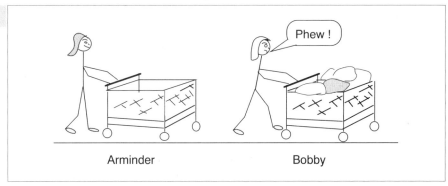

They both start to push their trolleys and wish to gain speed at the same rate. Who has to push the hardest? Clearly, Bobby. How much harder? Clearly, twice as hard. And so force must be proportional to mass.

Suppose now that Carla comes along and her trolley has the same load as Arminder's.

Figure 3.2

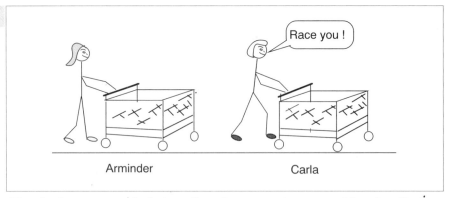

They both start to push their trolleys from a stationary position, but Carla pushes twice as hard as Arminder. What happens? Clearly Carla gains speed more rapidly – in fact, her acceleration will be twice as great. And so force must also be proportional to acceleration.

The rule is Force = mass × acceleration or $F = ma$, using standard symbols. It is known as Newton's Second Law.

> ### Newton's Second Law:
>
> ### Force = mass × acceleration

Example

An ice-yacht of mass 300 kg has an acceleration of 0.8 m s^{-2}. What force is needed to produce this?

Solution

A diagram is always helpful in answering these sorts of questions:

Figure 3.3

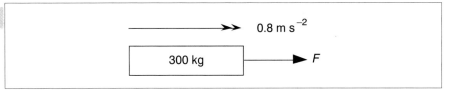

It is conventional to use double arrows for acceleration.

$\therefore$ $F = 300 \times 0.8 = 240$ $\therefore$ force needed = 240 N.

Example

A 6-tonne yacht is running before the wind. The wind produces a force of 350 N and the water a resistance of 50 N. Find the acceleration of the yacht.

Solution

Again, start by drawing a diagram:

Figure 3.4

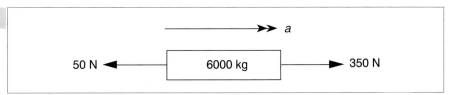

$\therefore$ $350 - 50 = 6000a \Rightarrow a = 0.05$ m s^{-2}

| Example | Six dogs pulling a 1500 kg sledge over level snow keep it going at constant speed. Eight dogs give it an acceleration of 0.3 m s⁻². With what force does each dog pull? |

Six dogs pulling a 1500 kg sledge over level snow keep it going at constant speed. Eight dogs give it an acceleration of 0.3 m s^{-2}. With what force does each dog pull?

Solution   Let force of each dog be D.

Figure 3.5

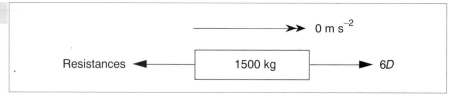

Steady speed $\Rightarrow$ no acceleration $\Rightarrow$ no overall force

$\therefore$ Resistances = $6D$.

With eight dogs we have:

Figure 3.6

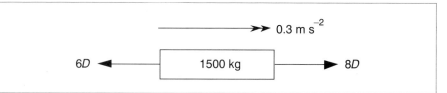

(The sledge will experience the same resistances, whatever the number of pulling dogs.)

$\therefore$ $8D - 6D = 1500 \times 0.3 \Rightarrow D = 225$

$\therefore$ Each dog has a pulling force of 225 N.

You should now be able to answer Exercises 1 to 16 on pp. 34–36.

Connected particles

These types of problem might involve a car pulling a caravan, or a train pulling a string of coaches, or a rope slung over a beam, with weights at either end. The method is the same in all cases – you write down the separate equations (using $F = ma$) and then solve them.

But before we begin, we need to look a little more closely at the tension in a rope (or string). Suppose that two teams are entered in a tug-of-war and they are both pulling with a total force of 2000 N.

Figure 3.7

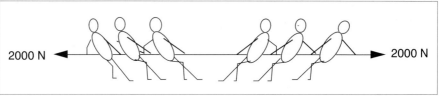

Clearly these teams are evenly matched and they are not going to move. Each team is being held back by the forces in the rope. Since both teams are pulling forwards with 2000 N, the force holding them back in the rope must also be 2000 N. And so the forces on the rope are:

Figure 3.8

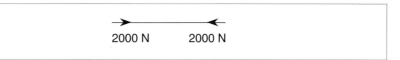

∴ The tension at either end of the rope is the same (in this case, 2000 N).

In general, then, **if a rope is taut, the tension at either end will be the same**. Even if it is slung over a beam, providing the beam is smooth, the tensions at either end will still be the same.

Example

A car of mass 900 kg tows a caravan of mass 700 kg. If the driving force from the engine is 320 N, find the force transmitted through the towbar and the acceleration of the car.

Solution

Here, too, we start by drawing a diagram:

Figure 3.9

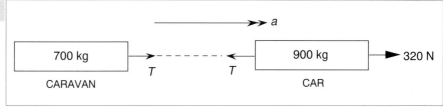

(Let *T* be the tension, the same at either end.)

Now use $F = ma$ on the car and caravan separately.

Caravan: $T = 700a$ ①
Car: $320 - T = 900a$ ②

Solve ① and ② simultaneously and get $T = 140$, $a = 0.2$

∴ The force is 140 N and the acceleration 0.2 m s^{-2}

When solving, it's nearly always easiest to just *add the equations*. In this case this gives us:

$$320 = 1600a, \text{ and so } a = 0.2. \text{ Then substitution back gives } T.$$

<table>
<tr><td>**Example**</td><td>A truck of mass 50 kg can run smoothly on horizontal rails. A light, inextensible rope is attached to the front of the truck, and this runs parallel to the rails until it passes over a light, smooth running pulley; the rest of the rope hangs down a vertical shaft, and carries a 10 kg load attached to the other end. Find the tension in the rope and the acceleration with which the truck and the load move. Comment on the modelling assumptions made.</td></tr>
</table>

Solution   A question written out like this sounds complicated. In examinations, however, you are likely to be given a diagram. Even if you are not, you can construct one of your own that models the situation.

And so we have:

Figure 3.10

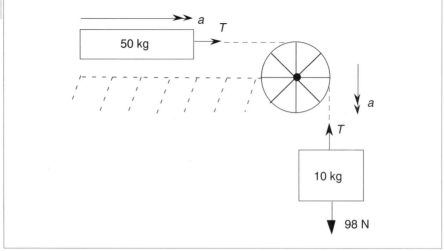

(The tensions, T, at either end of the rope are the same. The weight of the 10 kg load is $10 \times 9.8 = 98$ N.)

Truck: $T = 50a$ ①

Load: $98 - T = 10a$ ②

Now add ① and ② to get $a = 1.63$ (2 d.p.).   ∴ Acceleration = 1.63 m s^{-2}

Substitute back and get $T = 81.7$ (1 d.p.)   ∴ Force = 81.7 N

As for the assumptions made, comments might include the following:

● The truck and load are assumed to be particles.

● There is assumed to be no air resistance.

● The acceleration due to gravity is taken as being constant.

● In real life a perfectly smooth surface would be impossible.

● We have assumed that the rope is weightless, although in reality it would be bound to have some mass.

Example   Masses of 3 kg and 4 kg are joined by a string, which is placed over a light, smoothly-running pulley so that one mass hangs vertically on either side. Find the acceleration with which the larger mass descends and the tension in the string.

Solution   Here is a diagram of this set-up:

Figure 3.11

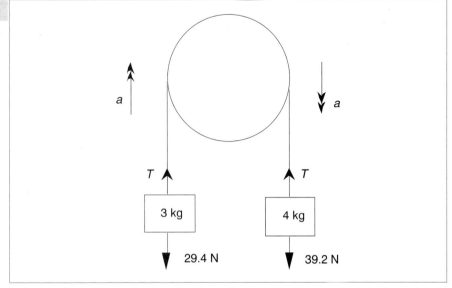

(The tension, T, at either end of the string is the same. The separate weights are: $4 \times 9.8 = 39.2$ N and $3 \times 9.8 = 29.4$ N.)

$\therefore$ $39.2 - T = 4a$ ... ①

$T - 29.4 = 3a$ ... ②

Add and get $a = 1.4$ m s^{-2}

Substitute back and get $T = 33.6$ N

You should now be able to answer Exercises 17 to 24 on pp. 36–38.

Practice questions

When you feel confident about the topics covered in this section, work through Exercises 25 to 27 on p. 39. They will give you a chance to revise the work covered so far and to practise some 'A' level type examination questions.

EXERCISES

1

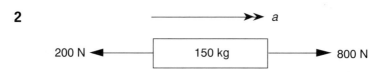

(a) Find acceleration *a*.

(b) If it starts from rest, what is its speed after 4 seconds?

2

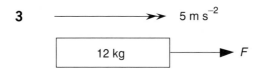

(a) Find acceleration *a*.

(b) If the initial speed is 4 m s⁻¹, what is its speed after 3 seconds?

3

(a) Find force *F*.

(b) If it is initially at rest, what distance is covered in the first 4 seconds?

4

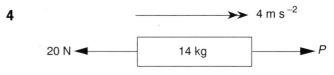

What is force *P*?

5

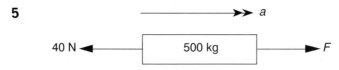

Moving at a steady speed:

(a) What is *a*?

(b) What is *F*?

6

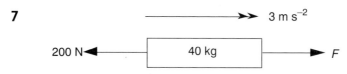

Moving at a steady speed:

(a) What is *a*?

(b) What is *P*?

(c) If *P* is suddenly removed, what is the retardation?

7

(a) What is *F*?

(b) When *F* is removed, what is the retardation?

8

Pull of the engine is *F* and resistances to motion are 20 N.

Initially the body is at rest. Force *F* = 120 N is applied for 6 seconds and then removed. How long will it be before the speed gets back to 2 m s^{-1}? (Talent required for this question!)

9

20 kg

Pull of engine is *F* and resistances to motion are 80 N. Initially the body is at rest. Force *F* = 120 N is applied for 10 seconds and then removed. How long before it is back to rest and what will be the total distance covered?

10 A 400 tonne train crashes into the buffers at 18 km h^{-1} and depresses them 1.25 m, before coming to rest. What is the force of impact of the train on the buffers?

11 A brick of mass 3 kg falls through water with an acceleration of 2 m s^{-2}. Find the resistance force.

12 A 2-tonne lorry is being lowered into the hold of a ship. Find the force in the cable if the lorry has:

(a) an acceleration of 0.5 m s^{-2} downwards

(b) a constant velocity of 3 m s^{-1}

(c) a retardation of 0.8 m s^{-2}.

13 The tension in a cable raising a load with an acceleration of 2.5 m s^{-2} is 6 N. What is the load?

14 A bottle of mass 0.5 kg is released from a submarine and rises to the surface with an acceleration of 0.8 m s^{-2}. If the water offers a resistance of 0.4 N, what is the force of buoyancy forcing it upwards?

15 A balloon which weighs 1 tonne is drifting horizontally. What is the total upwards vertical force on the balloon? If 100 kg of ballast are thrown out, with what acceleration does the balloon begin to ascend?

16 A balloon which weighs 600 kg is drifting horizontally. Some ballast is then thrown out so that the balloon begins to accelerate upwards at 0.2 m s^{-2}. How much ballast was thrown out?

17

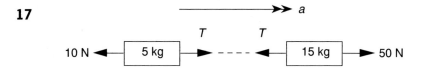

Find a and T.

18

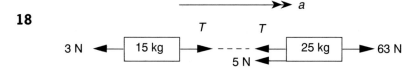

Find a and T.

19

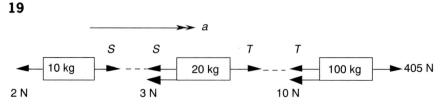

Find a, T and S.

20 Find *a* and *T* from the information given in the diagram below.

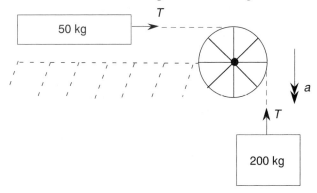

(Don't forget to put the weight in first!)

21 Find *a* and *T* from the information given in the diagram below.

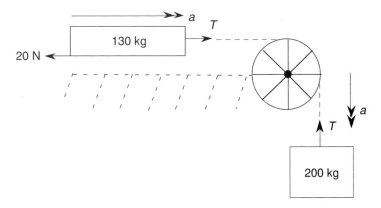

22

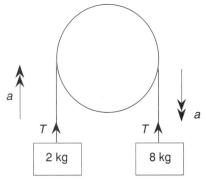

Find *a* and *T*

(Don't forget to put the weights in first!)

23 Find T and the missing mass.

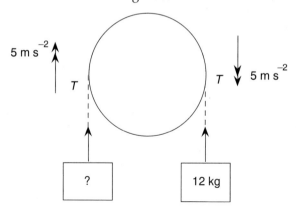

24

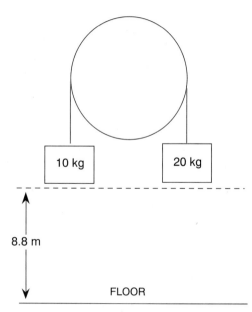

Weights released from rest when both are 8.8 m above the floor. The connecting chord snaps after 1.2 seconds so that the 20 kg mass falls freely to the floor.

(a) What is the speed of the 20 kg mass when it hits the floor?

(b) For how long does it fall freely?

(c) What *further time* elapses before the 10 kg mass hits the floor?

25 Two particles of mass $2m$ and $4m$ respectively are connected by a light inextensible string which passes over a smooth fixed pulley. The particles are released from rest with the parts of the string on each side of the pulley hanging vertically.

Find, in terms of g and m as appropriate:

(a) the magnitude of the acceleration of the particles

(b) the force exerted by the string on the pulley.

26 A light inextensible string passes over a small fixed smooth pulley. The string carries a particle of mass 0.06 kg at one end and a particle of mass 0.08 kg at the other end. The particles move in a vertical plane, with both hanging parts of the string vertical. Find the magnitude of the acceleration of the particles and the tension in the string.

27 (a) A 20 kg mass at the end of a cable is lowered at 2 m s^{-2}. What is the tension in the cable?

(b) A 30 kg mass at the end of a cable is lowered at a steady speed. What is the tension in the cable?

(c) A 40 kg mass at the end of a cable decelerates at 3 m s^{-2}. What is the tension in the cable?

SUMMARY

In this section you have looked at what happens when forces are in motion. In particular you have investigated the connection between force, mass and acceleration. You have applied what you learnt in a variety of situations – including some involving connected particles. Throughout you have applied modelling techniques – we hope that by now you are getting the hang of these and can see how useful they are.

You should now know that:

● forces are measured in newtons

● steady speed in a straight line means no acceleration (and so no overall force)

● tensions at either end of a taut rope are the same

● Weight = mass × acceleration due to gravity or $W = mg$

● Force = mass × acceleration or $F = ma$

You should also be able to:

● tackle problems involving connected particles

● model real life situations in this context, e.g. a car pulling a caravan would be modelled by two particles joined by a light inextensible string.

4

Equilibrium and friction

INTRODUCTION If you put a brick on a plank of wood inclined at 10° to the horizontal, it probably wouldn't slide off. However, if you raised one end of the plank, you would increase the angle of inclination. A point would come at which the brick would begin to slide. In this section we shall be looking at sliding and when it occurs.

When you have finished this section, you should be able to:

- find the resultant of two forces
- resolve a force in two perpendicular directions
- find normal reactions
- understand what is meant by coefficient of friction
- find the maximum frictional force available in any problem
- tackle questions involving equilibrium of particles
- tackle questions involving both motion and friction.

Combining two perpendicular forces

Let's suppose that two dogs are fighting over a 1.5 kg bone. The first is pulling due North, with a force of 3 N, and the other due East, with a force of 4 N.

Figure 4.1

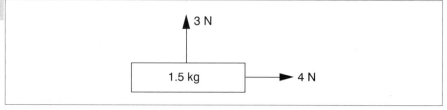

To find out which direction the bone moves, we 'follow the arrows':

Figure 4.2

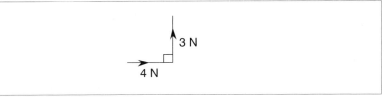

The hypotenuse will then give us the resultant force and lead to the direction of motion.

Figure 4.3

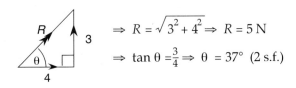

$$\Rightarrow R = \sqrt{3^2 + 4^2} \Rightarrow R = 5\,\text{N}$$

$$\Rightarrow \tan\theta = \tfrac{3}{4} \Rightarrow \theta = 37° \ (2\ \text{s.f.})$$

And so the bone is really being pulled by a single force of 5N on a bearing of 053°. We can go on to find its acceleration, using $F = ma$:

$$\therefore \qquad 5 = 1.5a \Rightarrow a = 3\tfrac{1}{3} \quad \therefore \ \text{Acceleration} = 33\tfrac{1}{3}\,\text{m s}^{-2}$$

You need to be able to find the resultant of two forces and so, before carrying on, spend some time working through a few practice questions.

You should now be able to answer Exercises 1 to 4 on p. 52.

Resolving a force in two perpendicular directions

We have just seen, with the example of the two dogs and their bone, that:

Figure 4.4

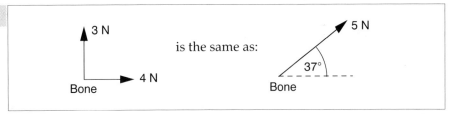

We've now got to be able to do the process in reverse. We need to go:

Figure 4.5

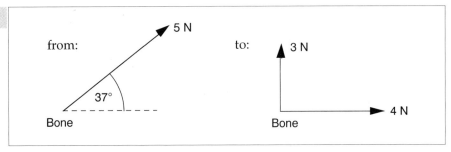

This process is called resolving a force in perpendicular directions. It is a *very important idea* indeed.

Example   A force of 25 N acts at an angle of 30° with the axis Ox as shown. Find its resolved parts in the direction of the x- and y-axes.

Figure 4.6

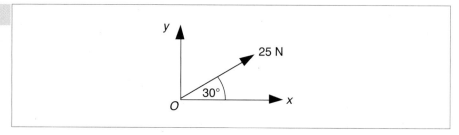

Solution   Begin by drawing a right-angled triangle.

Figure 4.7

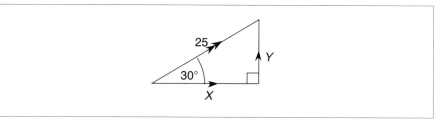

$$\therefore \quad \cos 30° = \frac{X}{25} \Rightarrow X = 25 \cos 30° \Rightarrow X = 21.7 \text{ (1 d.p.)}$$

$$\text{and} \quad \sin 30° = \frac{Y}{25} \Rightarrow Y = 25 \sin 30° \Rightarrow Y = 12.5$$

Therefore, we can now say that:

Figure 4.8

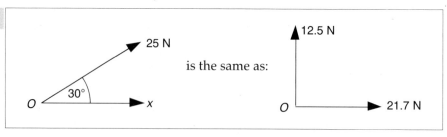

| **Example** | Find the horizontal and vertical components of the force shown below. |

Figure 4.9

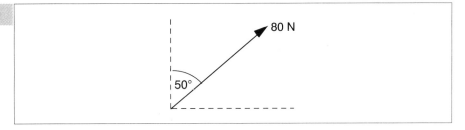

| **Solution** | Begin by drawing a right-angled triangle. |

Figure 4.10

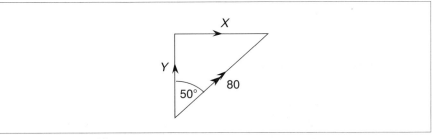

$\therefore \qquad \cos 50° = \dfrac{Y}{80} \Rightarrow Y = 80 \cos 50° \Rightarrow Y = 51.4 \ (1 \text{ d.p.})$

$\therefore \qquad$ The force in the northerly direction = 51.4 N

$\text{and} \qquad \sin 50° = \dfrac{X}{80} \Rightarrow X = 80 \sin 50° \Rightarrow X = 61.3 \ (1 \text{ d.p.})$

$\therefore \qquad$ The force in the easterly direction = 61.3 N

You should now be able to answer Exercises 5 to 8 on pp. 52–53.

The resultant of any number of forces

We can now use the previous methods to find the resultant of two forces which aren't perpendicular. Indeed, we can now find the resultant of any number of forces. All we have to do is to find their resolved components and then use Pythagoras.

Example   Find the resultant, in magnitude and direction, of the following forces:

Figure 4.11

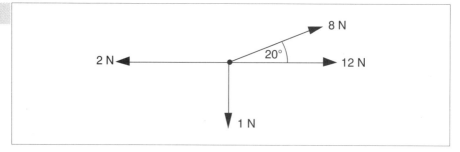

Solution   We begin by finding the resolved components of the 8 N force:

Figure 4.12

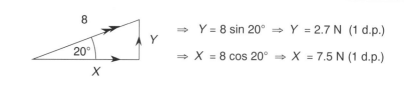

$\Rightarrow Y = 8 \sin 20° \Rightarrow Y = 2.7$ N (1 d.p.)

$\Rightarrow X = 8 \cos 20° \Rightarrow X = 7.5$ N (1 d.p.)

∴ The total force in the easterly direction is:

$$12 + 7.5 - 2 = 17.5 \text{ N}$$

and the total force in the northerly direction is:

$$2.7 - 1 = 1.7 \text{ N}$$

∴ The above four forces reduce to:

Figure 4.13

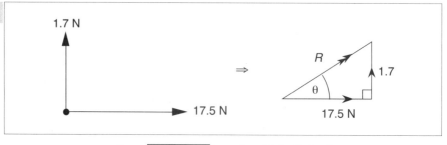

$$\Rightarrow R = \sqrt{17.5^2 + 1.7^2} \Rightarrow R = 17.6 \ (1 \text{ d.p.})$$

$$\text{and} \tan \theta = \frac{1.7}{17.5} \Rightarrow \theta = 6° \ (1 \text{ s.f.})$$

∴ The resultant force is 17.6 N inclined at 6° to the positive *x*-axis.

You should now be able to answer Exercises 9 to 12 on pp. 53–54.

The normal reaction

Suppose you have a mass of 80 kg and you stand, warming yourself, in front of the fire. Why doesn't your weight of 784 N (80 × 9.8) make you fall through the floor? It's because the floor is holding you up – it is pushing back with a force. But what force? Can it be more than 784 N? Clearly not, otherwise you would be taking off!

Figure 4.14

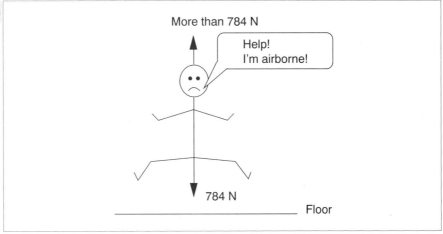

Can it be less than 784 N? Again, it clearly cannot be, otherwise you would be crashing through the floor-boards!

Figure 4.15

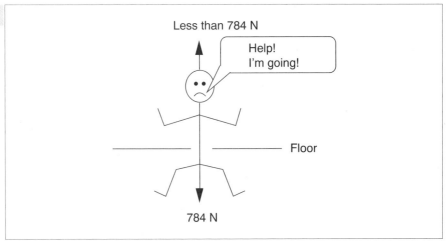

It must then be exactly 784 N.

Figure 4.16

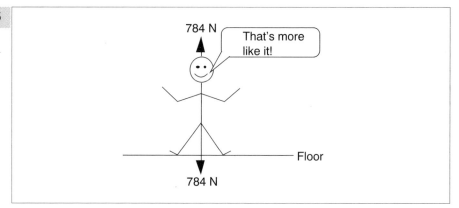

This supporting force from the floor (in this case, 784 N) is called **the normal reaction with the floor.**

This is an example of Newton's Third Law: this states that if a body Y (you) exerts a force on a body F (floor), then F exerts on Y a force **of the same magnitude acting along the same line but in the opposite direction.**

Example   A toy of mass 4 kg rests on the floor. What is the normal reaction?

A child now pushes this toy with a force of 10 N inclined at 40° to the horizontal. What is the normal reaction now?

Solution   The first part is easy.

Figure 4.17

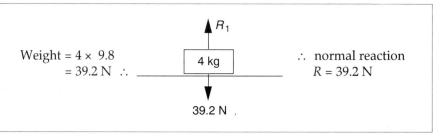

For the second part we have:

Figure 4.18

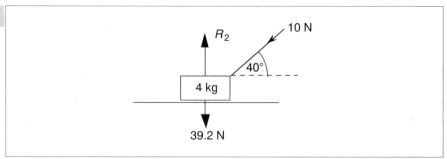

Common sense tells us that the supporting force R_2 must be greater than R_1. Let's find out what it is.

Firstly resolve the 10 N force in two directions:

Figure 4.19

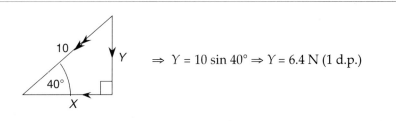

$\Rightarrow Y = 10 \sin 40° \Rightarrow Y = 6.4$ N (1 d.p.)

∴ total downwards force on the toy is:

39.2 + 6.4 = 45.6 N

∴ normal reaction $R_2 = 45.6$ N

You should now be able to answer Exercises 13 to 18 on pp. 54–55.

The coefficient of friction

When two surfaces touch, there may or may not be sliding – it all depends upon the roughness of the surfaces. If you incline a brick at 60° to the horizontal and then place another brick on top, the chances are that it won't slip. However, if you incline a pane of glass at 60° and then place another pane on top of that then, in all probability, it will start sliding. It's all because bricks are rougher than glass.

The amount of roughness between two surfaces is called **the coefficient of friction** and is usually denoted by the Greek letter μ (pronounced 'mew'). The bigger the value of μ, the rougher the surface. Metal surfaces, for example, have a value of μ of about 0.2 and very rarely do surfaces have μ bigger than 1.

The force of friction

As was said in the introduction, if you stand on a plank of wood which is inclined at 10° to the horizontal, you probably won't slide. This is because the frictional force is sufficient to hold you back. However, if you increase the angle of inclination, there will come a time when you will begin to slip. When you are on the point of slipping, the **frictional force is just enough to hold you** and you are said to be in **limiting equilibrium**. Beyond that, you slip away – the frictional force is no longer able to hold you.

The biggest frictional force available is μR, **when** R **is the normal reaction.** If the frictional force required is less than μR then you won't slip. Beyond that you will either be on the point of slipping or actually moving.

| **Example** | Consider the situation below where a 20 kg mass lies on a flat surface, with coefficient of friction μ. The horizontal force P is applied. |

Figure 4.20

What happens in the following cases:

(a) $\mu = 0.2$, $P = 30$ N   (b) $\mu = 0.5$, $P = 98$ N   (c) $\mu = 0.6$, $P = 120$ N?

| **Solution** | Let's use a diagram to illustrate what is going on here: |

Figure 4.21

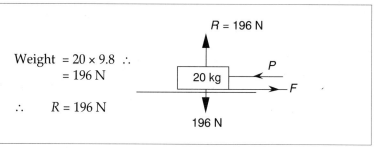

Weight $= 20 \times 9.8$ $\therefore$
$= 196$ N

$\therefore$ $R = 196$ N

(The frictional force F must act in the opposite direction from which the mass is tending to move.)

(a) $\mu = 0.2$ $\therefore$ Biggest frictional force available
$$= \mu R = 0.2 \times 196 = 39.2 \text{ N}$$

But P is only 30 N $\therefore$ Mass doesn't move.

(b) $\mu = 0.5$ $\therefore$ Biggest frictional force available
$$= \mu R = 0.5 \times 196 = 98 \text{ N}$$
But P is also 98 N $\therefore$ The mass will be on the point of moving.
It will be in limiting equilibrium.

(c) $\mu = 0.6$ $\therefore$ Biggest frictional force available
$$= \mu R = 0.6 \times 196 = 117.6 \text{ N}$$
But P is 120 N $\therefore$ the mass will begin to move under a total sideways force of $120 - 117.6 = 2.4$ N

$\therefore$ Using $F = ma$ we get $2.4 = 20a \Rightarrow a = 0.12$

$\therefore$ Mass accelerates away at 0.12 m s^{-2}

Example	Consider the situation below where a 40 kg mass lies on a flat surface, with coefficient of friction 0.6. A force P is applied at 30° to the horizontal. What is the least value of P if the mass is on the point of moving?

Figure 4.22

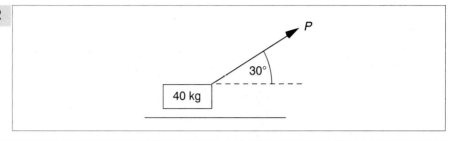

Solution	Resolve P in two directions, and put in the normal reaction R and the maximum frictional force $\mu R = 0.6R$. Not forgetting the weight $40 \times 9.8 = 392$ N, we get:

Figure 4.23

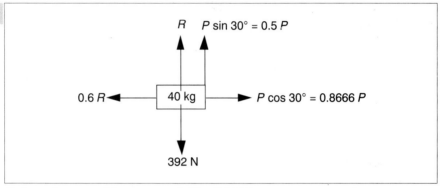

It doesn't move sideways ∴ $0.6R = 0.866P$ ... ①

This is called *resolving horizontally* and is usually written:

$(\rightarrow)$: $0.6R = 0.866P$ ... ①

It doesn't move vertically ∴ $R + 0.5P = 392$ ... ②

This is called *resolving vertically* and is usually written:

$(\uparrow)$: $R + 0.5P = 392$ ... ②

Now solve simultaneously to find P.

equation ② $\Rightarrow R = 392 - 0.5P$

∴   equation ① $\Rightarrow 0.6(392 - 0.5P) = 0.866P$

$\Rightarrow 235.2 - 0.3P = 0.866P$

$\Rightarrow 235.2 = 1.166P \Rightarrow P = 202$ (3 s.f.)

∴   Force $P = 202$ N.

Example   A mass of 50 kg is placed on a plane inclined at 60° to the horizontal. The coefficient of friction between the mass and the plane is 0.2. When the mass is released, what is its initial acceleration?

Solution   The weight = 50 × 9.8 = 490 N

Its component down the plane is 490 sin 60° = 424 N (3 s.f.) and its component perpendicular to the plane is 490 cos 60° = 245 N.

(Check back to Exercise 8 if you are unsure.)

Letting the normal reaction be R (so that the maximum frictional force is $\mu R = 0.2R$) we have:

Figure 4.24

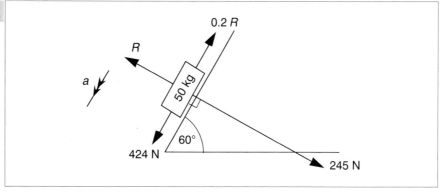

Resolving perpendicular to the plane: $R = 245$

∴ Force down the plane = $424 - 0.2R = 424 - 0.2 \times 245 = 375$ N

Now use $F = ma$ ∴ $375 = 50a \Rightarrow a = 7.5$

∴ Mass accelerates down the plane at 7.5 m s⁻².

Example   A particle of mass 40 kg lies on a rough plane inclined at 60° to the horizontal. A light inextensible string is attached to the particle and passes over a small smooth pulley fixed at the lip of the inclined plane. To the other end of the string is attached a particle of mass 80 kg, which hangs freely. The particles are released from rest with the string taut. If the coefficient of friction between the 40 kg mass and the plane is 0.5, find the initial acceleration of the system and the tension in the string.

Solution　The 40 kg mass has a weight of 392 N with components 392 sin 60° = 339 N
(3 s.f.) and 392 cos 60° = 196 N down and perpendicular to the plane
respectively.

(Refer back to Exercise 8, if you are unsure.)

Letting the normal reaction be R (so that the maximum frictional force is
$\mu R = 0.5R$) we have:

Figure 4.25

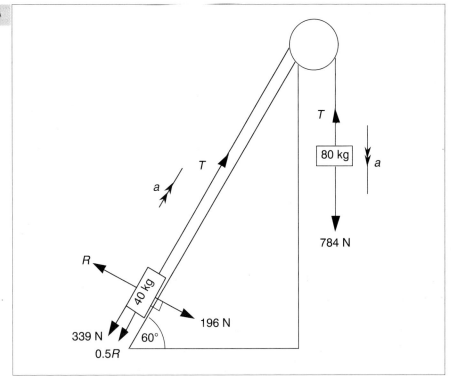

Resolving perpendicular to the plane: $R = 196$

∴ Maximum frictional force = $0.5R = 98$ N

∴ Total force down the plane = 339 + 98 = 437 N

∴ The two equations of motion are:

$$784 - T = 80a \qquad \qquad \dots ①$$
$$T - 437 = 40a \qquad \qquad \dots ②$$

Solve simultaneously and get acceleration $(a) = 2.89$ m s^{-2} (3 s.f.) and
tension $(T) = 553$ N (3 s.f.)

You should now be able to answer Exercises 19 to 26 on pp. 55–56.

Practice questions

When you feel confident about the topics covered in this section, work through Exercises 27 to 29 on pp. 56–57. They will give you a chance to revise the work covered so far.

EXERCISES

Find the resultant, in magnitude and direction, of the following sets of forces:

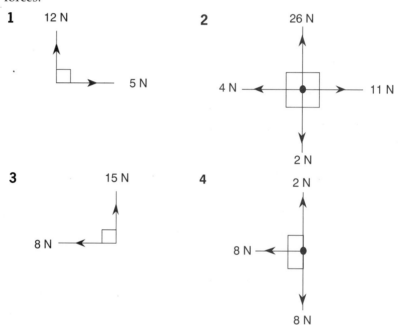

1   12 N   **2**   26 N
5 N   4 N   11 N
2 N

3   15 N   **4**   2 N
8 N   8 N
8 N

5 Resolve the following forces in the direction of the *x*- and *y*-axes:

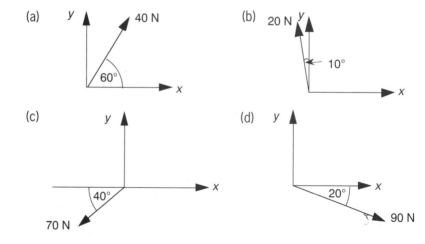

(a) *y*   40 N   (b) 20 N *y*
60°   10°
x   *x*

(c)   *y*   (d) *y*
40°   20°
x   *x*
70 N   90 N

6 Find the vertical and horizontal components of the forces shown below:

(a)

(b)

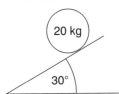

7 A particle of mass 20 kg rests on a plane inclined at 30° to the horizontal, as shown on the right:

What is the weight of the particle? What are the components of the weight (a) down the plane and (b) perpendicular to the plane?

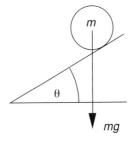

8 A particle of mass *m* rests on a plane inclined at θ to the horizontal, as shown on the right:

Write down the components of the weight

(a) down the plane and

(b) perpendicular to the plane.

In Exercises 9–12, find the resultant, in magnitude and direction, of the forces shown. (Give the direction as a bearing taking the *y*-axis or 'straight up' as due North.)

9

10

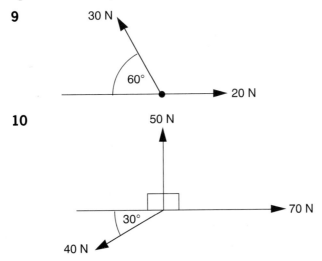

11

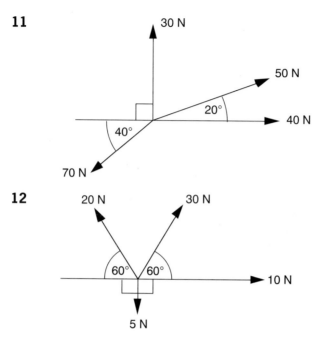

12

In Exercises 13 to 18, find the normal reaction R:

13

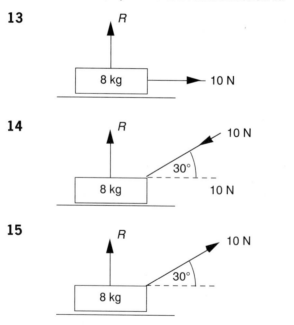

14

15

16

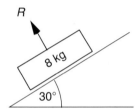

17

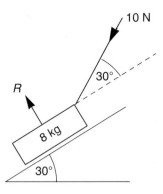

18

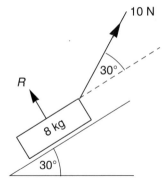

19 Consider the situation below where a 30 kg mass lies on a flat surface, with coefficient of friction μ. The horizontal force P is applied.

What happens in the following cases:

(a) $\mu = 0.5$, $P = 207$ N   (b) $\mu = 0.4$, $P = 110$ N?

20 A floor polisher of mass 5 kg is pushed along the floor at a steady speed; $\mu = 0.7$. If its handle (whose mass is negligible) is inclined at 35° to the horizontal, how hard must it be pushed in the direction of this handle?

21 An ice hockey puck of mass 0.2 kg is hit with a speed of 15 m s⁻¹ and travels 75 m before coming to rest. Find μ.

22 A sofa of mass 50 kg is dragged on to a van up a ramp at 25° to the horizontal. If $\mu = \frac{1}{3}$, what force parallel to the ramp is needed to pull it up at a steady speed?

23 A block of mass 30 kg can just be moved on a rough board by a horizontal force of 98 N. What is the coefficient of friction μ? What force will be needed to move the block if the direction of the force makes an angle with the horizontal of 30°

(a) upwards, (b) downwards?

24 A small body of mass 2 kg rests on a smooth plane inclined to the horizontal at an angle of 25°. The body is held in equilibrium by the pull of a string attached to it and inclined to the horizontal at 45°. Find the tension in the string and the normal reaction of the plane on the body.

25

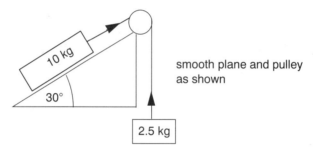

smooth plane and pulley
as shown

Find the acceleration of the system and the tension in the string.

26 Refer to the diagram in question 25 above. If the plane is now rough, what is the acceleration of the system when $\mu = 0.2$?

27 A particle, of mass M, is placed on a rough horizontal plane. The coefficient of friction between the particle and the plane is μ. A force of magnitude P, acting at an angle θ to the horizontal, is applied to the particle. Show that if this force is just sufficient to pull the particle along the plane, then:

$$P = \frac{Mg\mu}{\cos \theta + \mu \sin \theta}$$

28 A particle A, of mass $4m$, lies on a smooth plane inclined at $30°$ to the horizontal. A light inextensible string is attached to A and passes over a small smooth pulley P fixed at the top of the inclined plane. To the other end of the string is attached a particle B, of mass m, which hangs freely. The particles are released from rest with the string taut and with the portion AP parallel to a line of greatest slope of the inclined plane.

(a) Write down the equation of motion for particle A down the plane and the equation of motion for particle B.

(b) Hence calculate, in terms of m and g, the magnitude of the tension in the string and the acceleration of the particle A down the plane.

29

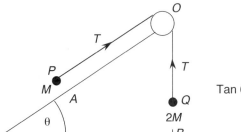

$\text{Tan } \theta = \dfrac{7}{24}$

A particle P, of mass M, is held at a point A on a rough plane inclined at an angle θ to the horizontal, where $\tan \theta = \dfrac{7}{24}$. The coefficient of friction between P and the plane is $\dfrac{11}{12}$. A light inextensible string, of length 50 cm, is attached to P and passes over a small smooth pulley O fixed at the top of the inclined plane. To the other end of the string is attached a particle Q, of mass $2M$, which hangs freely, and is vertically above a point B on the ground, as shown in the diagram above. The distances OA and OB are 32 cm and 43 cm respectively. The particles are released from rest in this position with the string taut and the portion OP parallel to a line of greatest slope of the inclined lane.

(a) Show that while the string is taut the acceleration of P up the plane is $\dfrac{7}{25} g$.

(b) Find the speed, in m s^{-1} to 2 s.f., with which Q hits the ground.

You should now be able to:

- find the resultant of two perpendicular forces by using Pythagoras' theorem
- resolve a force in two perpendicular directions using:

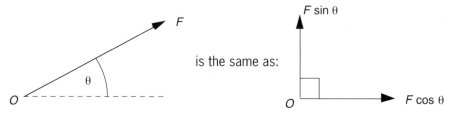

is the same as:

- quote from memory that the resolved components of a weight W on an inclined plane are given by:

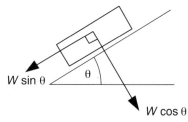

- quote from memory that the normal reaction R is perpendicular to the plane. And so:

and

- quote from memory that the maximum frictional force is μR, where μ is the coefficient of friction
- use the fact that the frictional force always opposes the direction of motion
- solve problems involving equilibrium or sliding, both on a horizontal plane and an inclined plane
- draw clear diagrams showing all relevant forces and accelerations.

5

Projectiles and variable acceleration

INTRODUCTION   If you throw a ball straight up in the air, you can use the equations of Section 2 to work out how high it will go. But if you don't throw it straight up, and throw it at an angle instead (as in cricket), how high will it reach then? In this Section you will find out how to answer that question.

In real life, of course, the wind will be blowing so that the cricket ball will be buffeted by variable air streams. The forces acting on the ball will therefore not be constant and so neither will its acceleration. Hence, since we cannot use the four constant acceleration equations, a totally new approach is required. This involves calculus – differentiation and integration – and in this section we'll be looking at some examples of variable acceleration.

When you have finished this section you should be able to:

● solve projectile problems (in a vertical plane under gravity)
● use the calculus to work out formulae for displacement, velocity and acceleration.

How to tackle projectile problems in two dimensions

Begin by writing down u v a s t in the two directions, one horizontally and one vertically.

$\therefore \rightarrow :$ u v a s t and $\uparrow :$ u v a s t

Horizontally there is no acceleration and so the u and v in that direction must always be the same. Vertically the acceleration will be -9.8 m s^{-2}. The times in the vertical table will be exactly the same as the times in the horizontal table:

$\therefore \rightarrow :$ u v a s t and $\uparrow :$ u v a s t

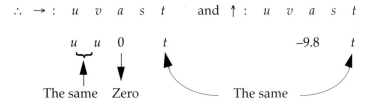

That gives you the general approach to take, except that if you want to find the direction in which a projectile is moving, you get its two velocity components and work from that:

Figure 5.1

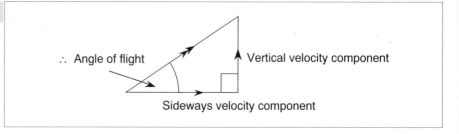

∴ Angle of flight

Vertical velocity component

Sideways velocity component

Example A golf ball, lying on a horizontal surface, is chipped into the air at 12 m s^{-1} at 60° to the horizontal. Find (a) the time taken to reach its maximum height (b) the maximum height (c) the time of flight (d) the range.

What is its speed, and what direction is it moving after $\frac{1}{2}$ second?

Solution

Figure 5.2

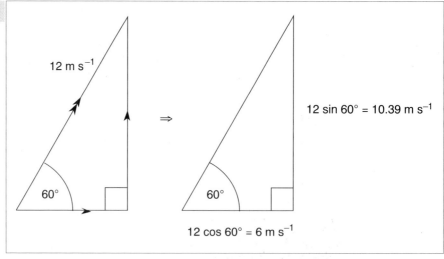

12 m s^{-1}

$\Rightarrow$

12 sin 60° = 10.39 m s^{-1}

60°

60°

12 cos 60° = 6 m s^{-1}

(Check with Section 4 if you've forgotten how to resolve.)

∴ → :

u	v	a	s	t
6	6	0		

and ↑ :

u	v	a	s	t
10.39		−9.8		

(a) The ball reaches maximum height when ↑ $v = 0$.

∴ Using $v = u + at \Rightarrow 0 = 10.39 - 9.8t \Rightarrow t = 1.06$

∴ The ball takes 1.06 seconds to reach maximum height.

(A practical tip: in tackling numerical questions, write down suitably rounded figures so that your methods are clear but, at the same time, use the memories in your calculator to get as accurate answers as possible. Once you've got an answer, round it off sensibly but, once again, keep the 'correct' answer in one of the memories.)

(b)   To find the maximum height we want $\uparrow s$.

$\therefore$ Using $s = \left(\dfrac{u + v}{2}\right)t \Rightarrow s = \left(\dfrac{10.39 + 0}{2}\right) 1.06 = 5.5$

$\therefore$ The maximum height is 5.5 m.

(c)   It takes as long to go up as it takes to come down.

$\therefore$ Its time of flight $= 2 \times 1.06 = 2.12$ seconds

(d)   To find the range we want $\rightarrow s$.

$\therefore$ Using $s = \left(\dfrac{u + v}{2}\right)t \Rightarrow s = \left(\dfrac{6 + 6}{2}\right) 2.12 = 12.7$

$\therefore$ Its range is 12.7 m.

After $\frac{1}{2}$ seconds, its $\uparrow v$ is given by $v = 10.39 - (9.8 \times \frac{1}{2}) = 5.49$ m s^{-1}

Since $\rightarrow v$ is always 6 m s^{-1} we therefore have:

Figure 5.3

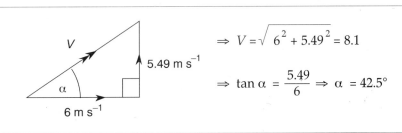

$\Rightarrow V = \sqrt{6^2 + 5.49^2} = 8.1$

$\Rightarrow \tan \alpha = \dfrac{5.49}{6} \Rightarrow \alpha = 42.5°$

$\therefore$ After $\frac{1}{2}$ second it is moving at 8.1 m s^{-1} at 42.5° to the horizontal (correct to 1 d.p.)

Example

An emergency relief aircraft releases its parcel of food supplies when descending at 20 m s^{-1} at an angle 30° to the horizontal. The parcel strikes the target 5 seconds later. At what height is the parcel released, and how far does the parcel travel horizontally?

Comment on the mathematical model that was used to solve this problem and name one factor that was ignored, but which would affect the result.

61

Solution   Look at the following diagram.

Figure 5.4

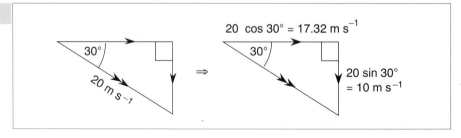

$$\therefore \rightarrow : \quad \begin{array}{ccccc} u & v & a & s & t \\ 17.32 & 17.32 & 0 & & 5 \end{array} \quad \text{and} \downarrow \quad \begin{array}{ccccc} u & v & a & s & t \\ 10 & & 9.8 & & 5 \end{array}$$

(Note that ↓ *a* is + 9.8 m s^{-2}.)

Find ↓ *s* using $s = ut + \frac{1}{2}at^2$

∴ $s = 10 \times 5 + \frac{1}{2} \times 9.8 \times 5^2 = 172.5$ m

∴   The parcel is released at a height of 172.5 m

Find → *s* using $s = \left(\frac{u + v}{2}\right)t$

∴ $s = \left(\frac{17.32 + 17.32}{2}\right)5 = 86.6$

∴   The horizontal range of the parcel is 86.6 m

The parcel was modelled as a particle.

Air resistance was ignored; in reality this would affect the result.

You should now be able to answer Exercises 1 to 7 on pp. 69–71.

Example OP represents a cliff 150 m high.

Figure 5.5

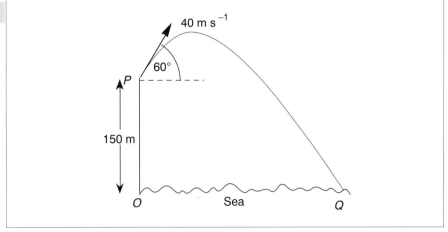

A ball is thrown from P with velocity 40 m s^{-1} at 60° to the horizontal. Find:

(a)   the greatest height of the ball above the sea

(b)   the time taken to hit the sea

(c)   the range OQ

(d)   the velocity at Q, in magnitude and direction.

Solution   First the useful diagram.

Figure 5.6

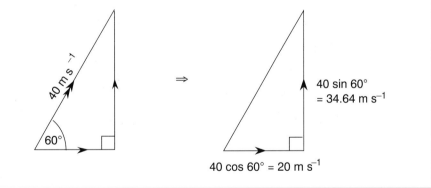

(a)   Reaches greatest height when ↑ $v = 0$

$\therefore$ Using $v^2 = u^2 + 2as$ $\Rightarrow$ $0^2 = 34.64^2 + 2 \times -9.8 \times s$

$$\Rightarrow \quad s = \frac{34.64^2}{2 \times 9.8} = 61.22$$

$\therefore$ The ball's greatest height above the sea = $150 + 61.22 = 211.22$ m.

(b) We *could* find the time taken to reach the greatest height and then add to it the time taken to fall back down into the sea. But there is a much cleverer way!

The initial velocity of the ball can be regarded as –34.64 m s^{-1} *downwards.*

∴   Starting from P we have:

↓ :	u	v	a	s	t
	–34.64		+ 9.8	+ 150	?

Using $s = ut + \frac{1}{2}at^2$ we get

⟹ $0 = 4.9t^2 - 34.64t - 150$

⟹ $t = \dfrac{34.64 \pm \sqrt{34.64^2 - 4 \times 4.9 \times - 150}}{2 \times 4.9}$ (using the quadratic

formula)

⟹ $t = 10.1$ or -3.0

∴   The ball takes 10.1 seconds to fly up to its highest point and then fall back down into the sea.

(c) To find OQ we want → s.

Using $s = \left(\dfrac{u + v}{2}\right) t$ we get $s = \left(\dfrac{20 + 20}{2}\right) 10.1 = 202$

∴   The range $OQ = 202$ m.

(d) To find ↓ v at Q we can use $v = u + at$

∴ $v = -34.64 + 9.8 \times 10.1$ (see table in (b))

∴ $v = 64.34$

Since → v is always 20 m s^{-1} we have at Q:

Figure 5.7

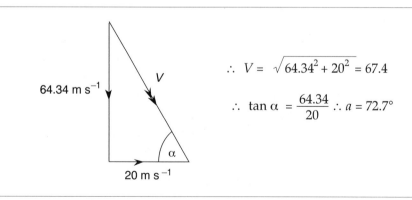

∴ $V = \sqrt{64.34^2 + 20^2} = 67.4$

∴ $\tan \alpha = \dfrac{64.34}{20}$ ∴ $a = 72.7°$

∴   Ball enters the sea at 67.4 m s^{-1} inclined at 72.7° to the horizontal.

Tackling projectile questions algebraically

In your examination you may be expected to derive general formulae for greatest height, time of flight and range. Let's see how this might be done.

Example

Figure 5.8

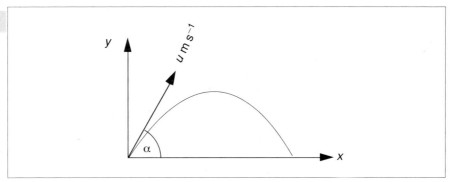

For the projectile illustrated above, prove that:

(a) the time of flight is $\dfrac{2\,u\sin\alpha}{g}$

(b) the greatest height reached is $\dfrac{u^2\sin^2\alpha}{2g}$

(c) the range is $\dfrac{2u^2\sin\alpha\cos\alpha}{g}$

Solution First the diagram.

Figure 5.9

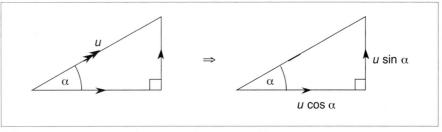

(a) The projectile reaches its highest point when $\uparrow v = 0$

Using $v = u + at$ we get $0 = u\sin\alpha - gt$

$\therefore$ Time to reach highest point $= \dfrac{u\sin\alpha}{g}$

$\therefore$ Time of flight $= \dfrac{2\,u\sin\alpha}{g}$

(b) Using ↑ $s = \left(\dfrac{u + v}{2}\right)t$ we get:

$$s = \left(\frac{u \sin \alpha + 0}{2}\right)\frac{u \sin \alpha}{g}$$

∴ $s = \dfrac{u^2 \sin^2 \alpha}{2g}$

∴   Greatest height reached $= \dfrac{u^2 \sin^2 \alpha}{2g}$

(c) Using → $s = \left(\dfrac{u + v}{2}\right)t$ we get:

$$s = \left(\frac{u \cos \alpha + u \cos \alpha}{2}\right)\frac{2\,u \sin \alpha}{g}$$

∴ $s = \dfrac{2u^2 \sin \alpha \cos \alpha}{g}$

∴   The range is given by $\dfrac{2u^2 \sin \alpha \cos \alpha}{g}$

(If you go on to study Module P2, you will see there that $2 \sin \alpha \cos \alpha$ can be more simply written as $\sin 2\alpha$. This means that the range is also given by $\dfrac{u^2 \sin 2\alpha}{g}$.)

Before you take your examination, I suggest that you have a glance through these proofs.

How to tackle problems involving variable acceleration

When the *acceleration varies we cannot use the four constant acceleration equations.* So what do we do?

We saw in Section 1 that the gradient of the distance–time graph gave us the velocity. But, if the acceleration varies then this distance–time graph will be a curve. To find the gradient of a curve at any point we have to differentiate. And so we have:

Figure 5.10

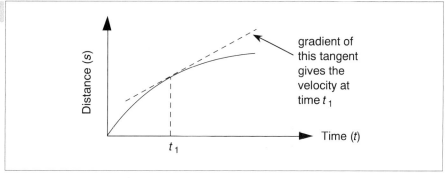

$$\therefore \quad \text{Velocity} = \frac{ds}{dt} = v$$

We also saw in Section 2 that the gradient of the velocity-time graph gave us the acceleration. And so we also have:

Figure 5.11

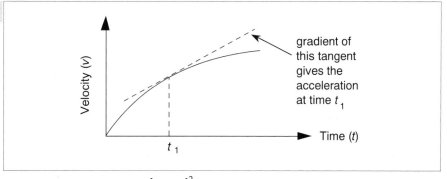

$$\therefore \quad \text{Acceleration} = \frac{dv}{dt} = \frac{d^2s}{dt^2}$$

And so, if we want to go from the velocity formula to the acceleration formula, we just differentiate. If we want to do it the other way round, i.e. go from the acceleration formula to the velocity formula, then we integrate (but don't forget + c!).

Let's summarise what we've got:

	Displacement $= s$	
Differentiate	Velocity $= \dfrac{ds}{dt} = v$	Integrate (and don't forget +c)
	Acceleration $= \dfrac{d^2s}{dt^2} = \dfrac{dv}{dt}$	

| **Example** | The velocity, v m s^{-1}, of a particle moving in a straight line t sec after the beginning of the motion is given by $v = 2 + 4t + t^3$. Find the initial acceleration. |

| **Solution** | $v = 2 + 4t + t^3 \Rightarrow$ acceleration $= \dfrac{dv}{dt} = 4 + 3t^2$ |

Initially $t = 0$ ∴ initial acceleration $= 4 + 0 = 4$ m s^{-2}.

| **Example** | The distance s metres moved by a particle travelling in a straight line in t sec is given by $x = 2t + t^3$. Calculate: |

(a) the average velocity over the first 3 seconds

(b) the velocity after 3 seconds.

| **Solution** | (a) $t = 3 \Rightarrow s = 2 \times 3 + 3^3 = 33$ |

∴ Particle covers 33 m in 3 seconds

∴ Average velocity $= 11$ m s^{-1}

(b) $v = \dfrac{dx}{dt} = 2 + 3t^2$

∴ $t = 3 \Rightarrow v = 2 + 3 \times 3^2 = 29$ ∴ Velocity $= 29$ m s^{-1}

| **Example** | A point moves in a straight line so that its acceleration in m s^{-1} is given by $f = t^2 + 2t$, where t is the time in seconds. If the initial velocity is 4 m s^{-1}, find the velocity after 3 seconds. |

| **Solution** | Acceleration $= \dfrac{dv}{dt} = t^2 + 2t$ |

Integrate and get $v = \dfrac{t^3}{3} + t^2 + c$

But $v = 4$ when $t = 0$ ∴ $c = 4$

∴   Velocity formula is $v = \dfrac{t^3}{3} + t^2 + 4$

∴ $t = 3 \Rightarrow v = \dfrac{3^3}{3} + 3^2 + 4 = 22$

∴   Velocity $= 22$ m s^{-1}

In this question f was used for acceleration (rather than a). You need to be aware of both notations.

Example	A train runs non-stop between two stations P and Q, and its velocity, t hrs after leaving P, is $60t - 30t^2$ km/h. Find the distance between P and Q.

Solution	Stops when $v = 0$ $\Rightarrow 60t - 30t^2 = 0$

$$\Rightarrow 30t(2 - t) = 0$$

$$\Rightarrow t = 0 \text{ or } 2$$

$\therefore$ The train takes 2 hours travelling from P to Q.

But   velocity $= \dfrac{dx}{dt} = 60t - 30t^2$

Integrate and get $x = 30t^2 - 10t^3 + c$

But $x = 0$ when $t = 0$ $\therefore c = 0$

$\therefore$ Distance formula is $x = 30t^2 - 10t^3$

$\therefore$ $t = 2 \Rightarrow x = 30 \times 4 - 10 \times 8 = 40$

$\therefore$ Distance between P and Q = 40 km

You should now be able to answer Exercises 8 to 17 on pp. 71–72.

Practice questions

When you feel confident about the topics covered in this section, work through Exercises 18 to 23 on pp. 73–74. They will give you a chance to revise the work covered so far.

EXERCISES

1

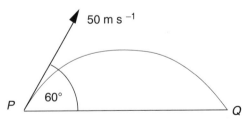

50 m s^{-1}

P 60° Q

An object is projected from P with velocity 50 m s^{-1} inclined at 60° to the horizontal PQ. Find:

(a) time of flight

(b) range PQ

(c) greatest height above PQ

(d) height above PQ after 2 seconds

(e) direction of flight after 3 seconds.

2 *OP* is a cliff 100 m high.

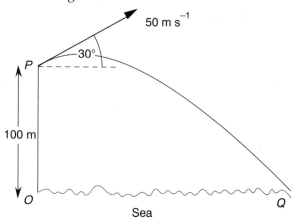

A ball is projected from *P* with velocity 50 m s⁻¹ at 30° to horizontal. Find:

(a) greatest height of ball above the sea

(b) time taken to hit the sea

(c) range *OQ*

(d) velocity at *Q*, in magnitude and direction.

3 OP is a cliff 100 m high.

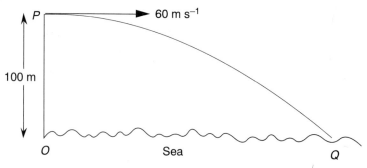

A ball is projected horizontally from *P* with velocity 60 m s⁻¹ . Find:

(a) time taken to hit the sea

(b) range *OQ*

(c) height above the sea after 2 seconds

(d) direction of flight after 3 seconds

(e) velocity after 3 seconds.

4

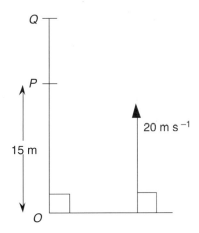

A ball is projected vertically upwards with velocity 20 m s⁻¹.
It just reaches Q and then falls back down again. Find:

(a)   time taken to reach P (where OP = 15 m)

(b)   time from P to Q

(c)   distance from P to Q

(d)   time ball is above P.

5   A jet of water leaves a hose-pipe with horizontal and vertical velocities
of 15 m s⁻¹ and 25 m s⁻¹. Find for how long each particle of water is in
the air, and how far the jet reaches.

6   A particle P is projected with speed u m s⁻¹ at an angle of elevation
θ where $\sin\theta = \frac{12}{13}$ from a point A on a horizontal plane. The particle
moves freely under gravity and strikes the horizontal plane at the
point B, where AB = 600 m.

(a)   Show that u = 91.

(b)   Calculate the greatest height reached by P above the horizontal
plane.

(c)   Calculate the time taken for P to reach B from A.

7   Find the range of a shell fired with muzzle velocity of 700 m s⁻¹ at 15°
to the horizontal.

8   Distance x at time t given by $x = 4t^3 + 8t + 2$.

Find the velocity and acceleration when t = 2.

9   Distance x at time t given by $x = 2t(t + 1)(t + 2)$.

Find the velocity and acceleration when t = 2.

10 The distance x at time t is given by $x = t^2 + t + 7$, when x is measured in metres and t in seconds. What is the velocity after 3 seconds? When does the velocity equal 9 m s^{-1}?

11 The acceleration of a particle is given by $f = 12t^2$, where f has units m s^{-2} and t is measured in seconds. After 1 second the velocity is 6 m s^{-1}. Find the velocity as a function of t. What is the initial velocity and when does the velocity equal 500 m s^{-1}?

12 The velocity of a particle in m s^{-1} is given by $v = 3t^2 - \frac{1}{3}t^3 + 9$, where t is measured in seconds. When does the acceleration equal zero? What is the distance covered between these two times?

13 A stopping train travels between two adjacent stations so that its velocity is v km/min, t minutes after leaving the first, where $v = \frac{4t}{3}(1 - t)$. Find:

(a) the average velocity for the journey in km/h

(b) the maximum velocity in km/h.

14 The formula connecting the velocity and time for the motion of a particle is $v = 1 + 4t + 6t^2$. Find the average velocity and the average acceleration for the interval $t = 1$ to $t = 3$, the units being metres and seconds.

15 A racing car starts from rest and its acceleration after t seconds is $(k - \frac{1}{6}t)$ m s^{-2} until it reaches a velocity of 60 m s^{-1} at the end of 1 minutes. Find the value of k, and the distance travelled in the first minute.

16 A particle starting from rest at O moves along a straight line OA so that its acceleration after t seconds is $(24t - 12t^2)$ m s^{-2}.

(a) Find when it again returns to O and its velocity, then,

(b) find its maximum displacement from O during this interval,

(c) what is its maximum velocity and its greatest speed during this interval?

17 P and R are two adjacent railway stations, and Q is a signal box on the line between them. A train which stops at P and R has a velocity $(\frac{3}{8} + \frac{1}{2}t - \frac{1}{2}t^2)$ km/min at t minutes past noon, and it passes Q at noon. Find:

(a) the times of departure from P and arrival at R

(b) an expression for the distance of the train from P in terms of t

(c) the average velocity between P and R, in km h^{-1}

(d) the maximum velocity attained, in km h^{-1}.

18 A stone thrown upwards from the top of a vertical cliff 56 m high falls into the sea 4 seconds later, 32 m from the foot of the cliff. Find the speed and direction of projection. (The stone moves in a vertical plane perpendicular to the cliff.)

19 A tile slides down a roof inclined at 30° to the horizontal starting 5 m from the edge of the roof. Assuming the roof is smooth find the horizontal distance from the edge of the roof that the tile hits the ground, if the edge of the roof is 8 m above the ground level.

20 A particle starts from rest at time $t = 0$ and moves in a straight line with variable acceleration f m/s², where

$$f = \frac{t}{5} \text{ for } 0 \le t < 5$$

$$f = \frac{t}{5} + \frac{10}{t^2} \text{ for } t \ge 5$$

t being measured in seconds. Show that the velocity is 2.5 m/s when $t = 5$ and 11 m/s when $t = 10$.

21 A particle moves in a straight line with a velocity of v m/s after t seconds, where $v = 3t^2 + 2t$. Find the acceleration at the end of 2 seconds, and the distance it travels in the 4th second.

22 A particle P moves from rest, at a point O at time $t = 0$ seconds, along a straight line. At any subsequent time t seconds, the acceleration of P is proportional to $(7 - t^2)$ m/s² and the displacement of P from O is s metres. The speed of P is 6 m/s when $t = 3$.

(a) Show that $s = \frac{1}{24} t^2 (42 - t^2)$

(b) Find the total distance, in metres, that P moves before returning to O.

23

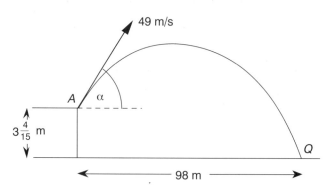

A golf ball is projected with speed 49 m/s at an angle of elevation α from a point A on the first floor of a golf driving range. Point A is at a height of $3\frac{4}{15}$ metres above horizontal ground. The ball first strikes the ground at a point Q which is at a horizontal distance of 98 m from the point A as shown in the above diagram:

(a) Show that $6\tan^2 \alpha - 30\tan \alpha + 5 = 0$.*

(b) Hence find, to the nearest degree, the two possible angles of elevation.

(c) Find, to the nearest second, the smallest possible time of direct flight from A to Q.

(*Hint: You will need to use the identities $\dfrac{\sin \alpha}{\cos \alpha} = \tan \alpha$

and $\dfrac{1}{\cos^2 \alpha} = 1 + \tan^2 \alpha$. You'll be meeting these identities 'officially' when you study Module P2)

SUMMARY

Having examined, in this section, the way all sorts of different objects travel when they are thrown, pushed or dropped, or fall off cliffs, you should now be able to:

● tackle two dimensional projectile questions, using the following layout:

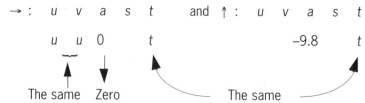

- work out the direction of flight, by working out the sideways and vertical components of velocity

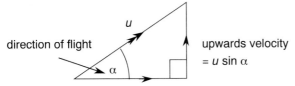

direction of flight

u

upwards velocity
= *u* sin α

α

sideways velocity = *u* cos α

- tackle variable acceleration problems by means of the following table:

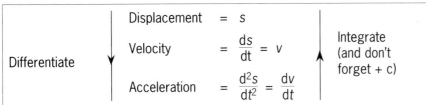

	Displacement = s	
Differentiate	Velocity = $\dfrac{ds}{dt}$ = v	Integrate (and don't forget + c)
	Acceleration = $\dfrac{d^2s}{dt^2}$ = $\dfrac{dv}{dt}$	

- find the *initial* velocity (find v when $t = 0$)
- find the *maximum* velocity (put acceleration = 0, find t and hence v)
- find the *average* velocity (divide the total displacement covered by the total time)
- find the *average* acceleration (divide the increase in velocity by the total time)
- recall that, when modelling projectile questions, you assume that the projectile is a particle and that there is no air resistance.

SECTION

6

Moments and centre of mass

INTRODUCTION If I gave you a saucer and asked you to balance it on your finger, you would do this by putting your finger under the centre of the saucer.

This centre is called the *centre of mass* of the saucer.

However, if you now put a biscuit over one end, where would you have to put your finger now in order to balance it?

It would certainly be a point away from the centre of the saucer and nearer the biscuit. Once the point has been found, that point would be the centre of mass of the saucer and biscuit. In this section we'll see how to set about finding balancing points for objects such as these.

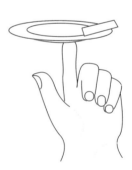

When you have finished this section you should be able to:

● work out the turning effect of a force – its moment
● use moments to solve see-saw problems
● tackle equilibrium problems involving laminas
● find the position of the centre of mass of one and two dimensional shapes
● work out angles when bodies are suspended in equilibrium.

The moment of a force

Suppose that a light rod is hinged at one end, A, and at the other end, B, there is applied a constant force of 20 N, always acting perpendicular to the rod AB. If the rod has length 4 m then we have:

Figure 6.1

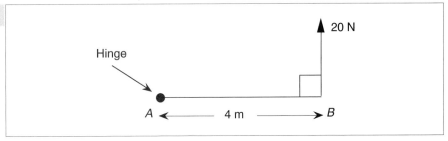

So what happens? Clearly the rod will spin around A. The 20 N force has a turning effect about A and this is called its moment about A. In this case the moment is:

$20 \times 4 = 80$ N m anti-clockwise.

In general, the moment of a force F about a point O is defined as $F \times d$, where d is the perpendicular distance of O from the line of action of F. If d is measured in metres and F in newtons, then Fd is measured in newton-metres or N m.

Figure 6.2

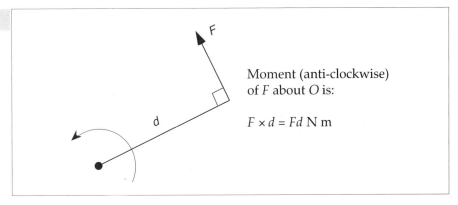

Moment (anti-clockwise) of F about O is:

$F \times d = Fd$ N m

Example   *ABCD* is a square of side 4 m. A force of 8 N acts along *BC* as shown.

Figure 6.3

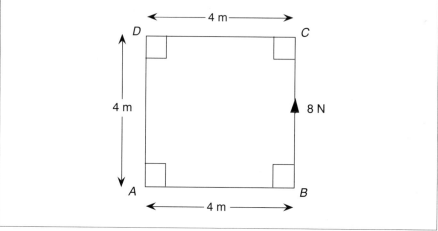

Find the moment of this force about: (a) *A*   (b) *D*   (c) *B*.

Solution   (a) $A\,\circlearrowleft$: $8 \times 4 = 32$ N m

($A\,\circlearrowleft$ is a short-hand way of saying 'the anti-clockwise moment about A'.)

(b) $D\,\circlearrowleft$: $8 \times 4 = 32$ N m

(c) $B\,\circlearrowleft$: 0 N m

(A force has no turning effect about a point that it passes through.)

Example   A force of 28 N acts as shown. What is its moment about *P*?

Figure 6.4

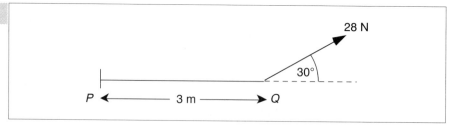

Solution   This resolves as follows (check back to Section 4, if you've forgotten about resolving):

Figure 6.5

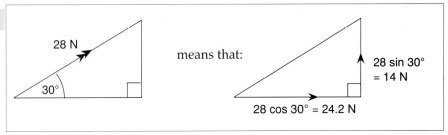

means that:

∴ We have:

Figure 6.6

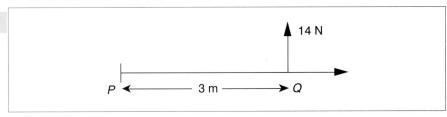

∴ $P\,\overset{\curvearrowleft}{}$: $3 \times 14 = 42$ N m

(The 24.2 N force has no moment about P since it passes through P.)

Example

Figure 6.7

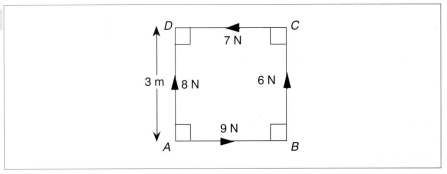

Square $ABCD$ of side 3 m. Forces act along the sides as shown. Find their total moment about: (a) A (b) B

Solution

(a) $A\,\overset{\curvearrowright}{}$: $6 \times 3 + 7 \times 3 = 39$ N m

(The forces 8 N, 9 N have no moment since they pass through A.)

(b) $B\,\overset{\curvearrowright}{}$: $7 \times 3 - 8 \times 3 = -3$ N m

(Since the 8 N has a clockwise turning effect about B, we need a negative sign.)

You should now be able to answer Exercises 1 to 4 on pp. 91–92.

Tackling equilibrium problems

A body is in equilibrium under a system of forces if it doesn't move. It must not move upwards, sideways or turn. And so, under a system of forces, given an equilibrium problem you:

● draw a clear diagram, and put in all the forces that are acting

● resolve upwards and get zero

● resolve across and get zero

● find the total moment about *any* point, and get zero.

The solution will then follow.

Example
The diagram shows a uniform rod PQ of mass 5 kg. The rod is 8 m long and is supported horizontally by two symmetrically placed strings attached at A and B.

Figure 6.8

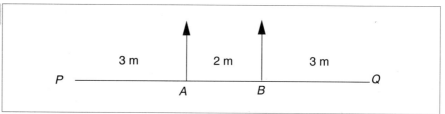

What are the tensions in the strings?

Solution
Rod PQ is uniform and so its centre of mass is in the middle of the rod. We therefore take the weight of the rod as acting through this centre. This gives

Figure 6.9

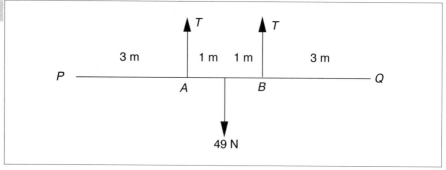

(The tensions T will be the same, since the system is symmetrical. The weight of the rod = 5×9.8 N or 49 N.)

$\uparrow : 2T = 49$ N $\quad \therefore T = 24.5$ N

The tension in each string is 24.5 N

Example

The diagram shows a non-uniform rod AB of weight 98 N. The rod is 2.2 m long and its centre of mass is 1.2 m from the end A. It is supported horizontally by two strings attached at A and C.

Figure 6.10

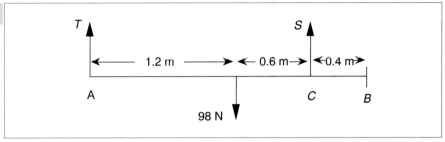

What are the tensions T and S?

Solution

$\uparrow : T + S = 98$ N   ...①

$A \circlearrowright : S \times 1.8 - 98 \times 1.2 = 0$ ...②

Equation ② gives $S = 65\frac{1}{3}$ N. Then ① gives $T = 32\frac{2}{3}$ N

Example

The diagram shows a uniform plank AE of length 6 m and weight 90 N. Anne weighs 500 N and sits at A. Brian also weighs 500 N and sits at B. Dusty the dog sits at D and the plank just balances horizontally.

Figure 6.11

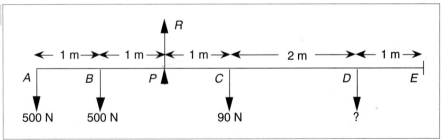

How much does Dusty weigh and what is the normal reaction R?

Solution

Let Dusty weigh W Newtons.

$\uparrow : R = 1090 + W$ ...①

$P \circlearrowright : 500 \times 2 + 500 \times 1 = 90 \times 1 + W \times 3$ ...②

(You can take moments about any point you like – I just fancied P!)

Equation ② gives $W = 470$ and ① gives $R = 1560$

$\therefore$ Dusty weighs 470 N. (That makes his mass $470 \div 9.8 = 48$ kg. Dusty must be a Great Dane!)

Example   A rod is hinged at *A*.

Figure 6.12

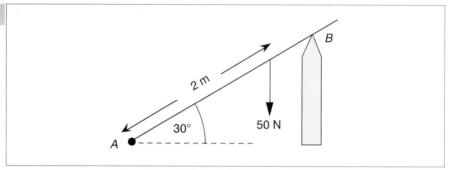

Calculate the distance *AB* if the smooth support at *B* exerts a force of 30 N on the rod.

Solution   The normal force of 30 N at *B* is at right angles to the rod.

Figure 6.13

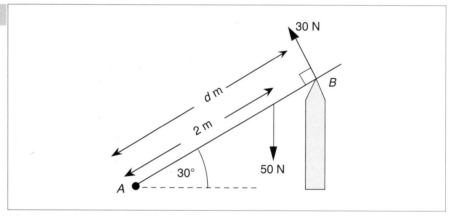

(Look at Exercises 13 to 18 in Section 4, if you need a reminder about normal reactions.)

The component of the 50 N weight perpendicular to *AB* is
50 cos 30° = 43.3 N. (See Section 4, Exercise 8 for a reminder.)

∴ *A* ↻ : 30 × *d* = 43.3 × 2 ⇒ *d* = 2.9 (1 d.p.)

∴ *AB* = 2.9 m (1 d.p.)

You should now be able to answer Exercises 5 to 14 on pp. 92–96.

Centre of mass of one-dimensional shapes

The centre of mass of any shape is the point about which it balances.

Suppose we are given a light rod AB of length 9 m with masses of 4 kg, 5 kg and 6 kg attached as shown.

Figure 6.14

One way of finding its centre of mass is to imagine a pivot point P put in.

Figure 6.15

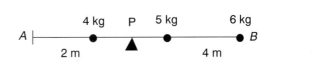

Now put in all the forces.

Figure 6.16

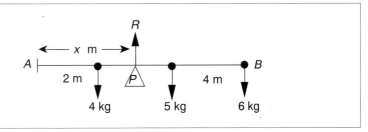

Resolving vertically we get $R = 15$ kg ...①

Then $A \curvearrowright$: 4 kg $\times 2 + 5$ kg $\times 5 + 6$ kg $\times 9 = 15$ kg $\times x$ (Using ①)

$\Rightarrow 4 \times 2 + 5 \times 5 + 6 \times 9 = 15 \times x$ ...(*)

$\Rightarrow x = 5.8$ m

$\therefore$ centre of mass of the system is 5.8 m from A.

A better way of finding its centre of mass is to go straight to equation(*)!

Set up a table of masses and distances (from point A).

	Separate masses			Total mass
Masses (kg)	4	5	6	15
Distance from A (m)	2	5	9	$\bar{x}$

Then just multiply as you go along.

$\therefore$ $4 \times 2 + 5 \times 5 + 6 \times 9 = 15\,\bar{x}$

$\therefore$ $\bar{x} = 5.8$ m, as before.

(It is conventional to use $\bar{x}$ rather than x when finding a centre of mass.)

Example   Find the centre of mass of the following system of particles.

Figure 6.17

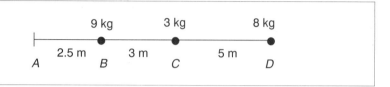

Solution

	B +	C +	D =	Whole thing
Masses (kg)	9	3	8	20
Distance from a (m)	2.5	5.5	10.5	$\bar{x}$

∴ $9 \times 2.5 + 3 \times 5.5 + 8 \times 10.5 = 20\bar{x}$

∴ $\bar{x} = 6.15$

∴   Centre of mass is 6.15 m from A.

Example   A cylindrical can is made of a metal of uniform density. The base radius is 3 cm and the height is 8 cm. It has a base but no lid.

Figure 6.18

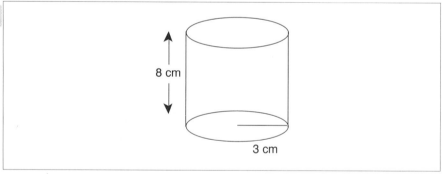

Find the height of the can's centre of mass.

Solution   Since it has uniform density, we can work with areas instead of masses.

	Base +	Curved surface	= Total
Area	9π	48π	57π
Height of centre of mass	0	4	$\bar{y}$

(Area of circular base $= \pi3^2 = 9\pi$; curved surface area $= 2\pi3 \times 8 = 48\pi$; centre of mass of the curved surface area must be half way up.)

∴ $9\pi \times 0 + 48\pi \times 4 = 57\pi \times \bar{y}$

$\therefore$ $0 + 192 = 57\,\bar{y}$ (divide through by π)

$\therefore$ $\bar{y} = 3.37$ (2 d.p.)

$\therefore$ Centre of mass is 3.37 cm above the base.

Example   A circular card of uniform density has centre O and radius 6 cm. A circular hole of radius 3 cm, and passing through O, is punched in the card.

Figure 6.19

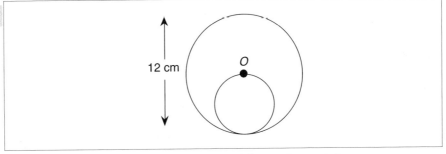

Find the position of the centre of mass of the card remaining.

Solution   The centre of mass of the shaded area lies on the axis of symmetry, the y-axis.

Figure 6.20

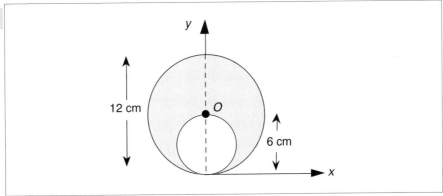

	Big circle	− Small circle	= Remaining card
Area	36π	9π	27π
y -coordinate of mass	6	3	$\bar{y}$

$\therefore$ $36\pi \times 6 - 9\pi \times 3 = 27\pi \times \bar{y}$

$\therefore$ $216 - 27 = 27\bar{y} \therefore \ \bar{y} = 7$

$\therefore$ Card has centre of mass 7 cm up the axis of symmetry.

You should now be able to answer Exercises 15 to 21 on pp. 96–97.

Centre of mass of two-dimensional shapes

With two-dimensional shapes *without an axis of symmetry*, you need two rows of distances. Otherwise it's the same as before.

Example	A 4 × 4 piece of card of uniform density with a 2 × 2 square removed from the top right-hand corner.

Figure 6.21

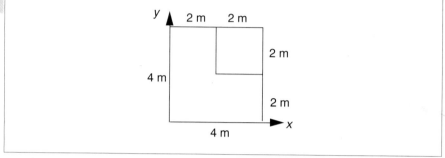

Find the coordinates of the centre of mass of the remaining card.

Solution

	Big square	−	Small square	=	Wanted shape
Area	16		4		12
x-coordinate (m)	2		3		$\bar{x}$
y-coordinate (m)	2		3		$\bar{y}$

∴ $16 \times 2 - 4 \times 3 = 12\,\bar{x}$

∴ $\bar{x} = 1\frac{2}{3}$ m. Similarly $\bar{y} = 1\frac{2}{3}$ m.

∴ The coordinates of the centre of mass are $(1\frac{2}{3}, 1\frac{2}{3})$.

Example	An L-shaped card of uniform density. Find the coordinates of its centre of mass.

Figure 6.22

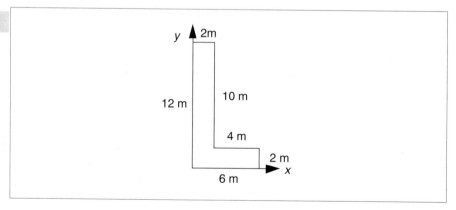

Solution   Separate into two areas A and B as shown.

Figure 6.23

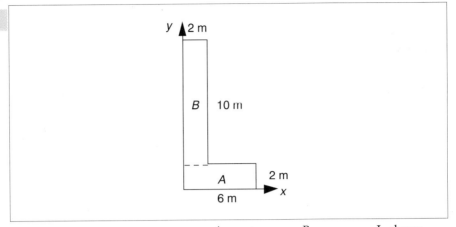

	A	+	B	=	L-shape
Area	12		20		32
x-coordinate (m)	3		1		$\bar{x}$
y-coordinate (m)	1		7		$\bar{y}$

∴ $12 \times 3 + 20 \times 1 = 32\bar{x}$ ⇒ $\bar{x} = 1.75$ m

∴ $12 \times 1 + 20 \times 7 = 32\bar{y}$ ⇒ $\bar{y} = 4.75$ m

∴   The centre of mass has coordinates (1.75,4.75).

Example   Find the centre of mass of lengths of wire of uniform density bent into the shape of the previous example.

Solution

Figure 6.24

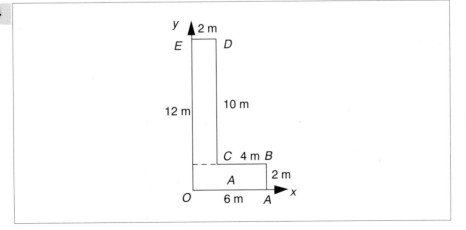

Since the wire is of uniform length, we work with lengths rather than masses.

	$OA +$	$AB +$	$BC +$	$CD +$	$DE +$	$EO =$	Whole thing
Length	6	2	4	10	2	12	36
x-coordinate (m)	3	6	4	2	1	0	$\bar{x}$
y-coordinate (m)	0	1	2	7	12	6	$\bar{y}$

$\therefore\ 6 \times 3 + 2 \times 6 + 4 \times 4 + 10 \times 2 + 2 \times 1 + 12 \times 0 = 36\,\bar{x} \qquad \therefore\ \bar{x} = 1\tfrac{8}{9}\,\text{m}$

$\therefore\ 6 \times 0 + 2 \times 1 + 4 \times 2 + 10 \times 7 + 2 \times 12 + 12 \times 6 = 36\bar{y} \qquad \therefore\ \bar{y} = 4\tfrac{8}{9}\,\text{m}$

$\therefore$ The centre of mass has coordinates $(1\tfrac{8}{9}, 4\tfrac{8}{9})$.

You should now be able to answer Exercises 22 to 24 on pp. 97–98.

Bodies hanging in equilibrium

In an earlier example we found the position of the centre of mass G of a 4×4 card with a 2×2 square removed from it. Our results were:

Figure 6.25

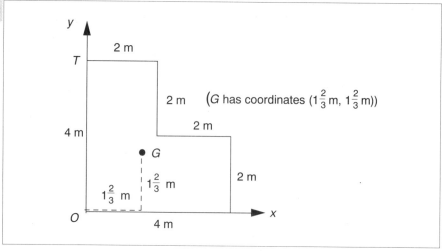

(G has coordinates $(1\tfrac{2}{3}\,\text{m}, 1\tfrac{2}{3}\,\text{m})$)

If this card is now suspended from the corner T, and allowed to hang freely, then G will swing round until it becomes vertically below T.

We will then have:

Figure 6.26

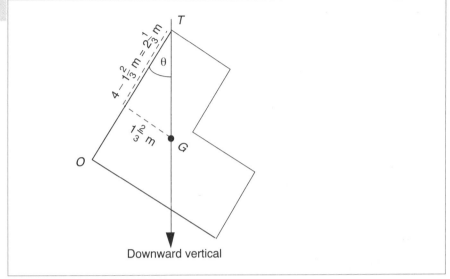

Downward vertical

∴   The angle that the edge *TO* makes with the downward vertical is given by:

$$\tan \theta = \frac{1\frac{2}{3}}{2\frac{1}{3}} \Rightarrow \theta = 35\frac{1}{2}^{\circ}$$

Easy enough, you may say, but the drawing of the second diagram could be tricky. The way you overcome this problem is to *take the first diagram, join T to G, and say that TG then represents the downward vertical.* And so:

Figure 6.27

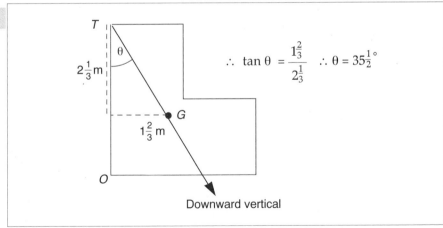

$$\therefore \quad \tan \theta = \frac{1\frac{2}{3}}{2\frac{1}{3}} \quad \therefore \theta = 35\frac{1}{2}^{\circ}$$

Downward vertical

The downward vertical is always obtained by joining the point of suspension to the centre of mass.

| **Example** | An L-shaped card of uniform density is freely suspended from *V*. |

Figure 6.28

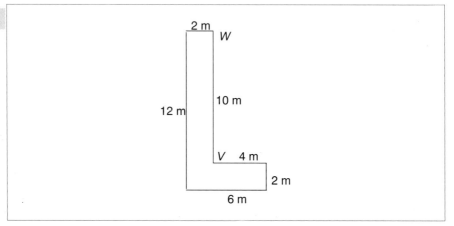

What angle does *VW* make with the downward vertical?

| **Solution** | An earlier example gave us the position of the centre of mass and so we have: |

Figure 6.29

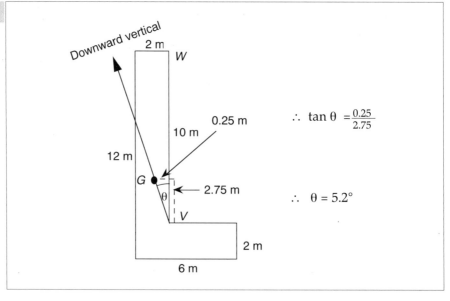

$$\therefore \quad \tan \theta = \frac{0.25}{2.75}$$

$$\therefore \quad \theta = 5.2°$$

You should now be able to answer Exercises 25 to 27 on p. 98.

Practice questions

When you feel confident about the topics covered in this section, work through Exercises 28–32 on pp. 98–99. They will give you a chance to revise the work covered so far.

EXERCISES

1

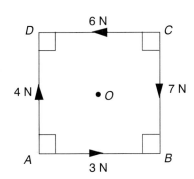

Square *ABCD* of side 4 m

Forces act along the sides as shown. Find their total anti-clockwise moment about:

(a)   *A*

(b)   *B*.

If *O* is the centre of the square, what is their total anti-clockwise moment about *O*?

2

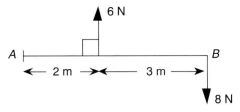

Light rod *AB* of length 5 m with forces as shown. Find their total anti-clockwise moment about:

(a)   *A*

(b)   *B*.

3

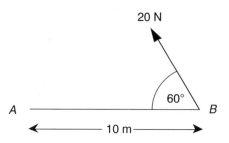

Force of 20 N acts as shown. Find its anti-clockwise moment about *A*.

4

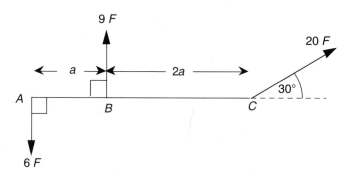

Light rod *AC* of length 3*a*. Forces act as shown. Find their total anti-clockwise moment about:

(a)   *A*

(b)   *C*.

5   In parts (a), (b), (c) and (d), find the unknown forces. In each case the pivot is marked with a cross. (Units are newtons and metres throughout.)

(a)

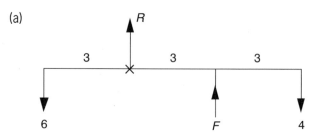

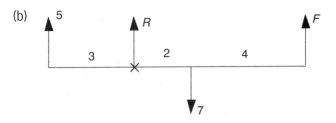

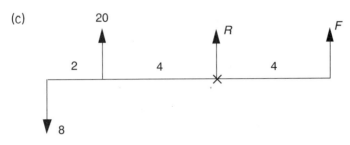

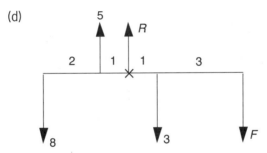

6 A uniform shelf of mass 15 kg and length 4 m is hinged at the left end. It is supported at a point 1m from the right end. What is the supporting force? If an additional mass of 15 kg is hung from the right end, what does the supporting force become?

7 A girder of negligible mass and length 4 m is suspended in a horizontal position by vertical cables attached at points 0.8 m and 2.4 m from one end. From that end is suspended a mass of 6 tonnes, and from the other a mass of 5 tonnes. Find the tensions in the cables.

8 A uniform beam 3 m long has weights 20 N and 30 N attached to its ends. If the weight of the beam is 50 N find the point on the beam where a support should be placed so that the beam will rest horizontally.

9 In parts (a), (b) and (c) the diagrams show an object in equilibrium. Calculate the forces indicated (units are newtons and metres throughout).

(a)

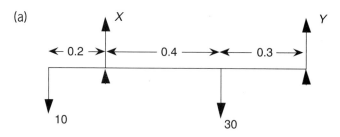

Find X and Y.

(b)

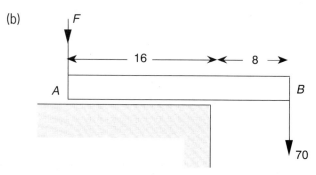

AB is a uniform plank weighing 100 N. Find the least force *F* required to prevent the plank overturning.

(c)

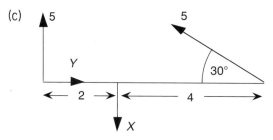

Find X and Y.

10

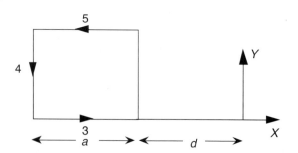

The diagram shows a set of forces in equilibrium.

Find X, Y and d.

11

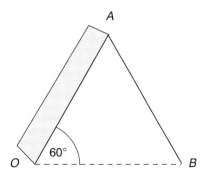

A loft door *OA* of weight 100 N is propped open at 60° to the horizontal by a light strut *AB*. The door is hinged at *O*.
If *OA* = *OB* = 1.2 m and the weight of the door acts through *C* where *OC* = 0.4 m, find the force in the strut.

12 The plunger of a pump is pulled vertically upwards, being attached to a point *A* of a lever *ABC*, which is pivoted at *B*. If *AB* = 0.2 m, *BC* = 1.2 m, angle *ABC* = 120°, and *BC* makes 30° with the horizontal, find the force with which the plunger is pulled up by an effort of 200 N applied at *C* perpendicular to *BC*.

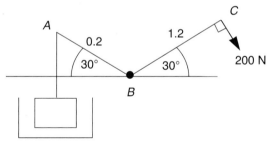

13 A uniform rod *AB* of weight *W* is hinged to a fixed point at *A*. It is held horizontally by a string at *B* as shown.

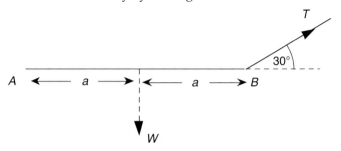

Find, in terms of *W*, the tension, *T*, in the string.

14

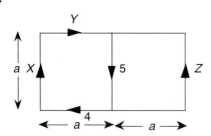

The system of forces shown is in equilibrium. Find X, Y and Z.

15

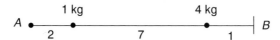

A uniformly heavy rod AB of mass 8 kg and length 10 m. Find the position of its centre of mass. (Hint: before you begin, mark in the point where the 8 kg acts.)

16 A straight rod AB of negligible mass has 3 masses fixed to it: 4 kg at A, 1 kg at a distance 24 cm from A and 5 kg at 40 cm from A. Find the distance of its centre of mass from A.

17 Imagine the x-axis. Find the centre of mass of 5 kg at $x = -4$, 3 kg at $x = 1$ and 2 kg at $x = 3$.

18 A cylindrical can of uniform density has a base but no lid. Its base radius is 5 cm and its height is 9 cm. Find the height of its centre of mass.

19

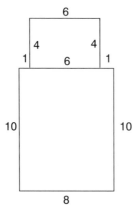

The illustrated 10 × 8 and 4 × 6 rectangles are both made of the same uniform material. Find the height of the centre of mass above the base. (Units in cm.)

20

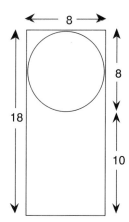

A rectangular card of uniform density is 8 × 18 and has a circular hole of radius 4 cm punched in it. Find the height of the centre of mass of the remaining card. (Units in cm)

21 Find the centre of mass of these bodies:

(a) a uniform cube of side 20 mm surmounted symmetrically by another cube of the same material of side 10 mm

(b) a conical tower of four children's bricks each a circular disc 1 cm thick, the radii of the discs being 4 cm, 3 cm, 2 cm, 1 cm. (All bricks are made of the same uniform material.)

22

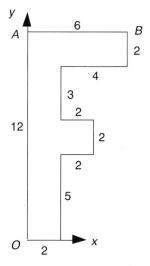

Find the coordinates of the centre of mass of the shown F-shaped card (assumed to be made of uniform material). (Units in cm.)

23 If the F-shape in question 22 is made instead from uniform bent wires, where is the centre of mass now?

24 *ABCD* is a uniform rectangular sheet of metal; *AB* = 100 mm and *BC* = 40 mm. Two circular holes are cut, each of radius 10 mm. One has its centre at the mid-point of *AC* and the other touches *BC* at its mid-point. Find the centre of mass of the remaining metal.

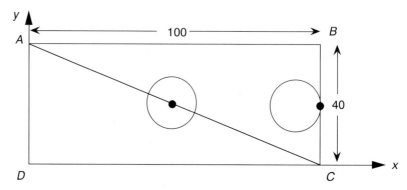

25 The F-shaped card in question 22 is suspended freely from *A*. What angle does *AO* make with the downward vertical?

26 The F-shaped wire in question 23 is suspended freely from *I*. What angle does *IH* make with the downward vertical?

27 The holed sheet in question 24 is suspended freely from *D*. What angle does *DC* make with the downward vertical?

28

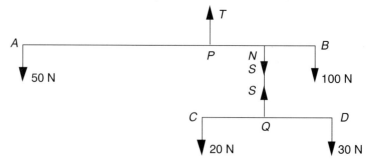

AB and *CD* are two light rods of lengths 11 m and 5 m respectively. The rod *AB* is suspended from point *P* by a vertical string under tension *T*. The rod *CD* is suspended from point *Q* by a vertical string *QN* under tension *S*; *N* is a point on *AB*. The rods *AB* and *CD* hang horizontally. If *AP* = 8 m, find:

(a) distance *CQ*   (c) distance *PN*

(b) tension *S*   (d) tension *T*.

29 A diving board of mass 150 kg is clamped at one end. A diver of mass 75 kg walks gently along the board, which is 3 m long. What turning effect is exerted on the clamp when the diver is:

(a) 1 m from the free end

(b) at the free end.

30 Four particles A, B, C, D of mass 3, 5, 2, 4 kg are at the points $(1, 6)$, $(-1, 5)$, $(2, -3)$, $(-1, -4)$. Find the coordinates of their centre of mass.

31

The figure shows a lamina which consists of a heavy uniform circular disc centre X and radius R from which a circular hole centre Y and radius r has been cut, where $r < R$. The centre of mass of the lamina is at a distance $4/9\, r$ from X and $XY = R - r$. By taking moments about X, or otherwise, show that $R = \dfrac{5r}{4}$.

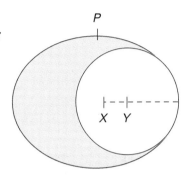

32

The figure shows an earring made from a uniform square lamina $ABCD$, which has each side of length 4 cm. Points X and Y are on the side BC and such that $BX = CY = 1$ cm. The square portion $XYUV$ is removed and the resulting earring is suspended from the corner A. The earring hangs in equilibrium.

The centre of mass of this earring is G.

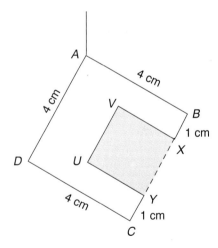

(a) State the distance, in cm, of G from AB.

(b) Find the distance, in cm, of G from AD.

(c) Find, to the nearest degree, the acute angle made by AD with the downward vertical.

ULEAC Mechanics M1 Specimen Paper 1994. Used with permission.

You should now be able to:

- find the moment of any force about any point

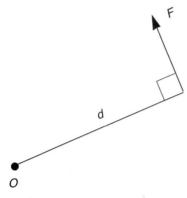

$$\therefore \; O\circlearrowright \; : F \times d$$

- tackle equilibrium problems by:
    - (a) resolving ↑ and getting zero
    - (b) resolving → and getting zero
    - (c) finding the total moment about *any* point and getting zero
- solve centre of mass problems by setting up a table and getting
  $$m_1x_1 + m_2x_2 + \dots = (m_1 + m_2 + \dots)\,\bar{x}$$
- work out angles when bodies are hanging in equilibrium. Remember that the line joining the point of suspension to the centre of mass will be the downward vertical.

7

Momentum and impulse

INTRODUCTION   While skating on an ice-rink at 3 m s⁻¹ you crash head-on with a friend skating at 2 m s⁻¹. Without stopping, you link arms and sail off together. But what will be your common speed? In this section we'll see how to answer such questions.

While skating on an ice-rink at 3 m s^{-1} you crash head-on with a friend skating at 2 m s^{-1}. Without stopping, you link arms and sail off together. But what will be your common speed? In this section we'll see how to answer such questions.

When you've finished this section you should be able to:

● work out momentum and impulse
● solve collision problems
● work out the loss of kinetic energy during a collision.

Momentum and impulse

If a mass m is subjected to a constant force F, its constant acceleration a is such that:

$$v = u + at \text{ and } F = ma.$$

(See Sections 2 and 3 if you need a reminder.)

Multiplying the first equation by m and then substituting for ma, we get:

$$mv = mu + Ft \text{ or } mv - mu = Ft \ldots \text{①}$$

The quantity, mass × velocity, is called the *momentum* of the body. Its units are in newton-seconds or Ns for short.

The quantity, force × time, is called the impulse of the force. Its units are also Ns.

momentum = mass × velocity

impulse = force × time

Impulse and momentum are measured in Ns

101

∴ equation ① can be re-written as:

momentum after – momentum before = impulse

or

change of momentum = impulse

Example	A 3 kg mass has a velocity of 5 m s^{-1}. What is its momentum?
Solution	Momentum = $3 \times 5 = 15$ N s
Example	A car of mass 1000 kg is pushed along a level road and acquires a speed of 2 m s^{-1} from rest in 10 seconds. What is the force pushing it?
Solution	Using the change of momentum approach: $1000 \times 2 - 1000 \times 0 = 10F$ ∴ The force $= 200$ N (An alternative method would be to work out the acceleration first of all – it's 0.2 m s^{-2} – and then use $F = ma$. However, this change in momentum approach is much quicker.)
Example	A hockey ball of mass 0.2 kg received an impulse of 1.2 N s at a free hit. With what speed does it begin to travel?
Solution	$0.2\,v - 0.2 \times 0 = 1.2$ ∴ $v = 6$ ∴ Speed $= 6$ m s^{-1}
Example	A hammer of mass 1.2 kg travelling at 15 m s^{-1} is brought to rest when it strikes a nail. What impulse acts on the hammer?
Solution	$1.2 \times 0 - 1.2 \times 15 =$ impulse ∴ Impulse $= 18$ N s (The negative sign implies that the impulse is towards the hammer.)

You should now be able to answer Exercises 1 to 6 on pp. 106–107.

Collisions: conservation of momentum

Suppose that masses m_1, m_2 are sliding along a smooth table with speeds u_1, u_2. They collide and then move off with speeds v_1, v_2 respectively. If the impulse during impact is I, then:

Figure 7.1

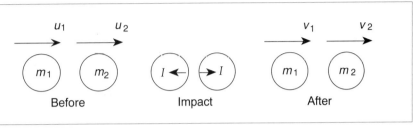

Before　　　　Impact　　　　After

Taking each mass separately we get:

$$m_2 v_2 - m_2 u_2 = I \quad \text{... ①}$$
$$m_1 v_1 - m_1 u_1 = -I \text{... ②}$$

Now add ① and ② and get (after rearrangement):

$$m_1 v_1 + m_2 v_2 = m_1 u_1 + m_2 u_2$$

∴ the total momentum afterwards equals the total momentum before

That is the only rule you need in order to solve collision problems in Module M1.

Example　A railway truck of mass 1500 kg travelling at 5 m s^{-1} hits another truck of mass 1000 kg which is stationary. The two trucks couple automatically and go on together. With what speed do they move?

Solution　A diagram is always helpful:

Figure 7.2

Conservation of momentum ⇒

$$1500 \times 5 + 1000 \times 0 = 2500 \times v \Rightarrow v = 3 \therefore \text{speed} = 3 \text{ m s}^{-1}$$

Example	A truck of mass 225 kg is moving at 3 m s⁻¹. A man of mass 75 kg runs straight towards it and meets it head-on at a speed of 6 m s⁻¹. If the man jumps on to the truck when he meets it, how fast and in what direction will the truck be moving afterwards?

Solution	Start with a diagram:

Figure 7.3

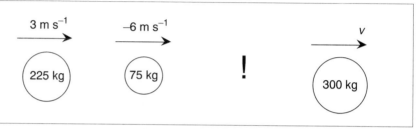

3 m s^{-1} -6 m s^{-1} v

225 kg   75 kg   !   300 kg

(Always get the speed arrows pointing in the same direction before you begin.)

$\therefore \quad 225 \times 3 - 75 \times 6 = 300v \Rightarrow v = 0.75$

$\therefore$ Truck will move in the same direction at 0.75 m s⁻¹

Example	When a toy truck of mass 240 grammes hits another stationary truck mass 360 grammes its speed is reduced from 4 to 1 m s⁻¹. What speed is given to the second truck?

Solution

Figure 7.4

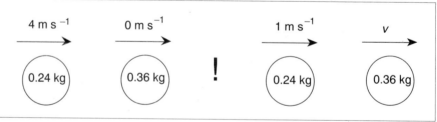

4 m s^{-1} 0 m s^{-1} 1 m s^{-1} v

0.24 kg   0.36 kg   !   0.24 kg   0.36 kg

$\therefore \quad 0.24 \times 4 + 0.36 \times 0 = 0.24 \times 1 + 0.36v \Rightarrow v = 2$

$\therefore$ The second toy truck gains a speed of 2 m s⁻¹

| Example | A mass of $3m$ with velocity $4u$ strikes a mass of m moving with a velocity u in the same direction. If they coalesce, find their subsequent velocity in terms of u. |

| Solution | |

| Figure 7.5 | 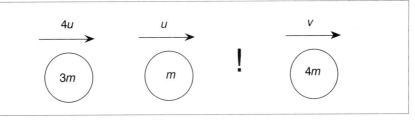 |

(Coalesce means 'join together'.)

$\therefore$ $3m \times 4u + m \times u = 4m \times v$

$\therefore$ $12u + u = 4v \Rightarrow v = 3.25u$

You should now be able to answer Exercises 7 to 16 on pp. 107–109.

Kinetic energy

When a body is in motion, the expression:

$$\tfrac{1}{2}\,\text{mass} \times (\text{velocity})^2$$

is called the *kinetic energy* of the body. Its units are in joules. (We'll return to this in more detail in Section 9.)

$$\text{kinetic energy} = \tfrac{1}{2}\,\text{mass} \times (\text{velocity})^2$$

| Example | A body of mass 5 kg moving initially with velocity 7 m s^{-1} has its velocity reduced to 3 m s^{-1}. Find the loss of kinetic energy. |

| Solution | K.E. before $= \frac{1}{2} \times 5 \times 7^2 = 122.5$ J |

                          K.E. after $= \frac{1}{2} \times 5 \times 3^2 = 22.5$ J

$\therefore$ Loss of K.E. $= 122.5 - 22.5 = 100$ J

(K.E. is an accepted shorthand for kinetic energy as is J for joules.)

<table>
<tr><td>Example</td><td>A body mass 2 kg velocity 4 m s⁻¹ strikes a body mass 3 kg moving with velocity 4 m s⁻¹ in the opposite direction. If the heavier body is brought to rest by the collision find:</td></tr>
</table>

A body mass 2 kg velocity 4 m s^{-1} strikes a body mass 3 kg moving with velocity 4 m s^{-1} in the opposite direction. If the heavier body is brought to rest by the collision find:

(a) the velocity of the lighter body after the collision and

(b) the total loss of kinetic energy as a result of the impact.

Solution

Figure 7.6

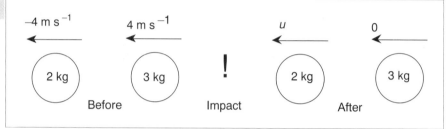

(a) Conservation of momentum gives
$$2 \times -4 + 3 \times 4 = 2 \times u + 3 \times 0 \implies u = 2 \text{ m s}^{-1}$$

(b) Total K.E. before $= \frac{1}{2} \times 2 \times 4^2 + \frac{1}{2} \times 3 \times 4^2 = 40 \text{ J}$

Total K.E. after $= \frac{1}{2} \times 2 \times 2^2 = 4 \text{ J}.$

∴ loss of K.E. $= 40 - 4 = 36 \text{ J}$

You should now be able to answer Exercises 17 and 18 on p. 109.

Practice questions

When you feel confident about the topics covered in this section, work through Exercises 19 to 20 on pp. 109–110. They are all are taken from past examination papers and will give you a chance to revise the work covered so far.

EXERCISES

1 In what time will a force of 8 N reduce the speed of a particle of mass 3 kg from 21 m s⁻¹ to 6 m s⁻¹?

2 A dart of mass 0.12 kg flying at a speed of 20 m s⁻¹ hits the dartboard and comes to rest in 0.1 seconds. What is the average force exerted by the dartboard on the dart?

3 A cup of 90 grammes is dropped from a height of 1.25 m. What impulse does it receive on striking the floor if it does not rebound?

4 A batsman receives a cricket ball of mass 160 grammes at a speed of 6 m s^{-1} and returns it straight back to the bowler at 12 m s^{-1}. What impulse does the bat give to the ball?

5 A coin of mass 5 grammes is shoved across a board. It receives an initial impulse of 0.01 N s and stops after sliding 0.5 m. Find the coefficient of friction.

6 Sand falls steadily through a hole on to a conveyor belt moving horizontally. 4 kg of sand falls every second, striking the belt at 10 m s^{-1}. Assuming that the sand does not bounce on impact, find the vertical force exerted by the belt on the sand.

7

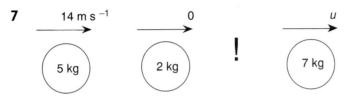

Find:

(a) u

(b) the impulse received by the 2 kg mass.

8

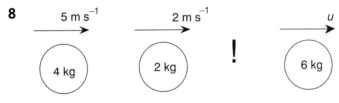

Find:

(a) u

(b) the impulse received by the 2 kg mass.

9

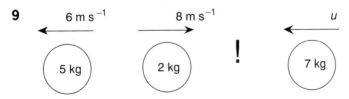

Find:

(a) u

(b) the impulse received by the 5 kg mass and

(c) the impulse received by the 2 kg mass.

10

Initially mass of 10 kg and 6 kg are at rest on a smooth horizontal surface. A force of 40 N is now applied to the 10 kg mass for 8 seconds and then removed. Later it coalesces with the 6 kg mass. Find

(a) the speed of the 10 kg mass after 8 seconds

(b) the distance covered by the 10 kg mass at that time

(c) the common speed of the combined mass after impact.

11

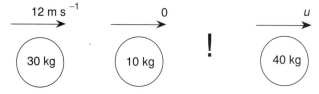

(a) Find the value of u.

(b) If a force of 20 N is then applied to the combined mass for 10 seconds, find the distance covered in that time (assuming no resistances).

12 A bullet is fired with a speed of 550 m s^{-1} into a block of wood of mass 0.49 kg, and becomes embedded in it. If it gives the block a speed of 11 m s^{-1}, find the mass of the bullet.

13 A 20 kg shell is travelling horizontally at 400 m s^{-1} when it explodes into two fragments of masses 8 kg and 12 kg. If the 12 kg fragment has a velocity of 700 m s^{-1} in the original direction of motion, find the velocity of the lighter fragment.

14 Two pails each of mass 3 kg are suspended at rest by a string passing over a smooth fixed horizontal bar. A brick of mass 1 kg is dropped into one of them from a height of 2.5 m. Find the initial velocity of the pails.

15 A bullet of mass m is fired with a horizontal speed $2u$ into a stationary block of wood of mass 50 m which is free to move horizontally.

Find the velocity of the block if:

(a) the bullet goes right through it and emerges with speed u

(b) the bullet becomes embedded in the block.

16 A vertical post of mass M is to be driven into the ground. A pile-driver of mass m strikes the post vertically with velocity v. Assuming that the pile-driver does not bounce off the post, prove that the velocity with which the post enters the ground is $mv/(M + m)$.

17 A body of mass 8 kg increases its speed from 4 m s^{-1} to 6 m s^{-1}. What is the gain in kinetic energy?

18 A body mass 225 kg velocity 4 m s^{-1} strikes a body mass 75 kg initially at rest. If the bodies move away together find:

(a) their common velocity

(b) the total loss of kinetic energy during the impact.

19

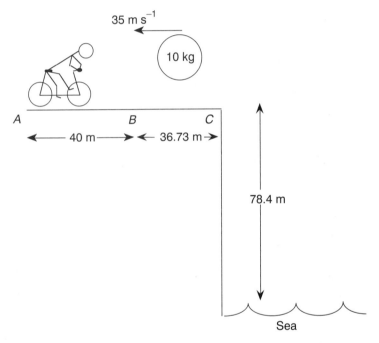

35 m s^{-1}

10 kg

A   B   C

40 m   36.73 m

78.4 m

Sea

A 70 kg cyclist on a 30 kg bike revs up from rest at A. His driving force on the bicycle is 696 N and the resistance to motion is 196 N.

(a)   What is the acceleration of the bicycle?

(b)   What is the cyclist's speed at B (40 m ahead of A)?

When the cyclist reaches B a 10 kg lump of soft clay hits him in the eyes and sticks to his goggles. At impact the clay is flying at 35 m s^{-1} towards the bicycle.

(c)   What is the speed of the cyclist after impact?

Not being able to see, he stops pedalling but, having no brakes, has to rely on friction to slow him down.

(d)   What is his retardation?

(e)   What is his speed when he reaches the cliff's edge at C (36.73 m from B)?

The bicycle now flies straight off the cliff's edge into the sea.

(f)   How long does it take him to hit the water?

(g)   How far out does he hit the sea?

(h)   What is his speed (in magnitude and direction) as he begins to sink?

(i)   How much kinetic energy has been gained from just before impact with the clay until he begins to sink?

20 A small sphere R of mass 0.08 kg, moving with a speed 1.5 m/s, collides directly with another small sphere S, of mass 0.12 kg, moving in the same direction with speed 1 m/s. Immediately after the collision R and S continue to move in the same direction with speeds u m/s and v m/s respectively. Given that $u : v = 21 : 26$

(a)   Show that $v = 1.3$

(b)   Find the magnitude of the impulse, in N s, received by R as a result of the collision.

SUMMARY

You should now know that:

- momentum = mass × velocity and it is measured in N s
- momentum after − momentum before = impulse
- impulse is measured in N s
- during collisions there is a conservation of total momentum

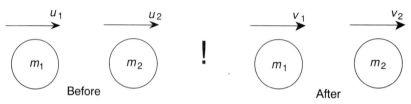

$$\Rightarrow m_1 u_1 + m_2 u_2 = m_1 v_1 + m_2 v_2$$

- kinetic energy = $\frac{1}{2}$ mass × (velocity)^2 and it is measured in J

- there is a loss of kinetic energy during any collision.

Vectors in mechanics

INTRODUCTION You already looked at vectors and vector notation in Section 1. In this section we shall move on to look at how to use vector methods in mechanics problems. Most of the work will involve tackling the material in the previous six sections in a slightly different way.

When you have finished this section you should be able to:

● use vectors in problems involving velocity, accelerations and forces.

● use differentiation and integration of vectors to solve variable acceleration problems

Velocity as a vector

Suppose that particle Q is moving and its components of velocity are 5 m s^{-1} in the direction of the positive x-axis and 6 m s^{-1} in the direction of the positive y-axis. The velocity vector of Q can then be written as $(5\mathbf{i} + 6\mathbf{j})$ m s^{-1}.

Acceleration as a vector

An acceleration vector such as $(7\mathbf{i} - 8\mathbf{j})$ m s^{-2} means that the components of acceleration are 7 m s^{-2} in the direction of the positive x-axis and 8 m s^{-2} in the direction of the negative y axis.

Force as a vector

If the resolved components of a force are (say) 9 N in the direction of the positive x-axis and 10 N in the direction of the positive y-axis, then this force can be written in vector form as $(9\mathbf{i} + 10\mathbf{j})$ N.

<table>
<tr><td>**Example**</td><td>A force **F** = (5**i** + 6**j**) N acts at a point P whose position vector is (3**i** + 3**j**) m. Find the moment of **F** about the point A whose position vector is (**i** + **j**) m.</td></tr>
</table>

Solution   It is always a good idea to have a diagram to look at.

Figure 8.1

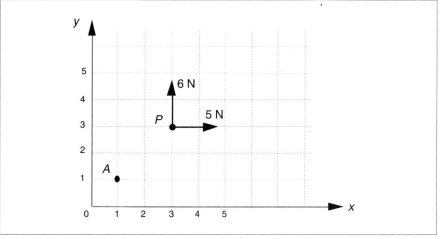

Once you have drawn a diagram, it's back to familiar methods (in this case they are familiar from Section 6).

$$\therefore A \circlearrowleft : 6 \times 2 - 5 \times 2 = 2\,\text{N m}$$

$\Rightarrow$ the anti-clockwise moment of **F** about A is 2 N m.

Example   A force **F** is given by (5**i** – 12**j**) N. What is the magnitude and direction of this force?

Solution

Figure 8.2

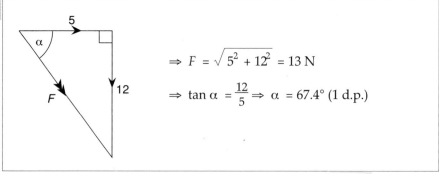

$$\Rightarrow F = \sqrt{5^2 + 12^2} = 13\,\text{N}$$

$$\Rightarrow \tan \alpha = \frac{12}{5} \Rightarrow \alpha = 67.4° \text{ (1 d.p.)}$$

$\therefore$ **F** has a magnitude of 13 N and acts on a bearing 157.4°.

(Unless stated otherwise, it will be assumed throughout that due North is along the positive y-axis and due East is along the positive x-axis.)

Example What is the magnitude of the velocity vector $(0.8\mathbf{i} - 0.6\mathbf{j})$ m s^{-1}?

Solution

Figure 8.3

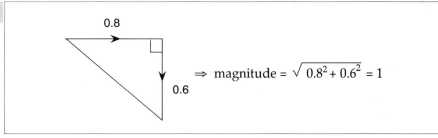

$\Rightarrow$ magnitude $= \sqrt{0.8^2 + 0.6^2} = 1$

A vector which has magnitude 1 is called a *unit vector*. (You'll meet this idea again in Exercise 29.)

Example A force $\mathbf{F}$ has magnitude 30 N and acts in the direction $3\mathbf{i} + 4\mathbf{j}$. Express $\mathbf{F}$ as a vector in component form.

Solution

Figure 8.4

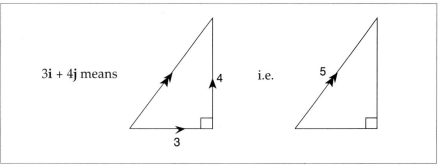

$3\mathbf{i} + 4\mathbf{j}$ means   i.e.

$\therefore$ $3\mathbf{i} + 4\mathbf{j}$ has magnitude 5.

But $\mathbf{F}$ is in this direction with magnitude 30 N.

Since $30 = 6 \times 5 \Rightarrow \mathbf{F} = 6(3\mathbf{i} + 4\mathbf{j}) = (18\mathbf{i} + 24\mathbf{j})$ N.

Example   A force **F** = (88**i** – 16**j**) N acts on a mass of 8 kg. Find the acceleration of the mass:

(a)   as a vector

(b)   in magnitude and direction.

Solution   **F** = *m***a** ⇒ 88**i** – 16**j** = 8**a** ⇒ 11**i** – 2**j** = **a**

∴   (a)   The acceleration vector is 11**i** – 2**j**.

(b)   Look at Figure 8.5.

Figure 8.5

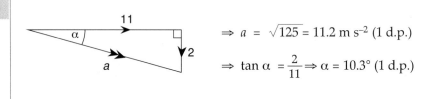

⇒ $a = \sqrt{125} = 11.2$ m s^{-2} (1 d.p.)

⇒ $\tan \alpha = \dfrac{2}{11} \Rightarrow \alpha = 10.3°$ (1 d.p.)

∴   **a** has magnitude 11.2 m s^{-2} and acts on a bearing 100.3°.

Example   A mass of 6 kg has velocity vector **v** = (4**i** + 3**j**) m s^{-1}. Find the momentum of the mass in vector form. What is its speed? What is its kinetic energy?

Solution   Momentum = *m***v** = 6(4**i** + 3**j**) = (24**i** + 18**j**) Ns.

Figure 8.6

Also **v** = 4**i** + 3**j** ⇒

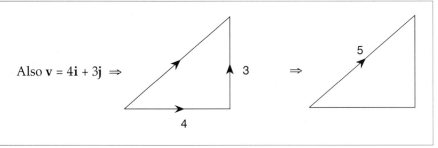

∴   Speed = magnitude of velocity vector = 5 m s^{-1}

∴   The kinetic energy = $\dfrac{1}{2} mv^2 = \dfrac{1}{2} \times 6 \times 5^2 = 75$ J

Example   A 3 kg mass with velocity vector (10**i** – 3**j**) m s^{-1} hits a 5 kg mass with velocity vector (2**i** + 21**j**) m s^{-1}. After impact they coalesce. Find:

(a)   their common velocity after impact

(b)   the total loss of kinetic energy

(c)   the impulse experienced by the 3 kg mass during impact.

Solution	(a) Conservation of momentum

$$\Rightarrow 3(10\mathbf{i} - 3\mathbf{j}) + 5(2\mathbf{i} + 21\mathbf{j}) = 8\mathbf{v}$$
$$\Rightarrow 40\mathbf{i} + 96\mathbf{j} = 8\mathbf{v} \Rightarrow \mathbf{v} = (5\mathbf{i} + 12\mathbf{j}) \text{ m s}^{-1}$$

(b) K.E. before $= \frac{1}{2} \times 3 \times (10^2 + 3^2) + \frac{1}{2} \times 5 \times (2^2 + 21^2) = 1276$ J

K.E. after $= \frac{1}{2} \times 5 \times (5^2 + 12^2) = 422.5$ J

$\therefore$ Loss of kinetic energy $= 1276 - 422.5 = 853.5$ J

(c) Momentum after – momentum before = impulse

$\therefore$ $3(5\mathbf{i} + 12\mathbf{j}) - 3(10\mathbf{i} - 3\mathbf{j}) = \mathbf{I}$

$\Rightarrow 15\mathbf{i} + 36\mathbf{j} - 30\mathbf{i} + 9\mathbf{j} = \mathbf{I}$

$\Rightarrow \mathbf{I} = (-15\mathbf{i} + 45\mathbf{j})$ Ns, the impulse on the 3 kg mass

Example A force of $(12\mathbf{i} - 8\mathbf{j})$ N acts on a 4 kg mass, which is initially at rest, at a point whose position vector is $(\mathbf{i} + 3\mathbf{j})$ m. Find the position vector of the mass after 10 seconds.

Solution $\mathbf{F} = m\mathbf{a} \Rightarrow 12\mathbf{i} - 8\mathbf{j} = 4\mathbf{a} \Rightarrow \mathbf{a} = 3\mathbf{i} - 2\mathbf{j}$

Now let's consider the motion in the x-direction ($\rightarrow$) and the y-direction ($\uparrow$):

$\rightarrow : u$	v	a	s	t	$\uparrow : u$	v	a	s	t
0		3		10	0		−2		10

$\therefore$ $\rightarrow : s = \frac{1}{2} \times 3 \times 10^2 = 150$ and $\uparrow : s = \frac{1}{2} \times -2 \times 10^2 = -100$

But mass was initially at $(\mathbf{i} + 3\mathbf{j})$ m.

$\therefore$ After 10 seconds it will be at $(1 + 150)\mathbf{i} + (3 - 100)\mathbf{j} = 151\mathbf{i} - 97\mathbf{j}$

Example The position vector of a particle at time t seconds is given by:

$$\mathbf{r} = (8t^3\mathbf{i} + t^4\mathbf{j}) \text{ m}$$

Find its velocity and acceleration after 2 seconds.

Solution Using the methods of Section 5, we differentiate to get the velocity vector. We could use any of the symbols $\mathbf{v}$, $\frac{d\mathbf{r}}{dt}$ or $\dot{\mathbf{r}}$ to represent this velocity vector but $\dot{\mathbf{r}}$ is the most common.

$\therefore$ Velocity vector $= \dot{\mathbf{r}} = 24t^2\mathbf{i} + 4t^3\mathbf{j}$

$\therefore$ $t = 2 \Rightarrow \dot{\mathbf{r}} = (96\mathbf{i} + 32\mathbf{j})$ m s^{-1}

Now differentiate again to get the acceleration vector (and $\ddot{\mathbf{r}}$ is the popular notation this time.)

$\therefore$ Acceleration vector $= \ddot{\mathbf{r}} = 48t\mathbf{i} + 12t^2\mathbf{j}$

$\therefore$ $T = 2 \Rightarrow \ddot{\mathbf{r}} = (96\mathbf{i} + 48\mathbf{j})$ m s^{-2}

| Example | A particle has velocity vector **v**, where **v** = $(2t\mathbf{i} + 3t^2\mathbf{j})$ m s^{-1}, at time t seconds. |

Example   A particle has velocity vector **v**, where **v** = $(2t\mathbf{i} + 3t^2\mathbf{j})$ m s^{-1}, at time t seconds.

Initially the particle is at a point whose position vector is $(\mathbf{i} + 4\mathbf{j})$ m.

Find the position vector of the particle at time t.

Solution   Using the methods of Section 5, we integrate to get the position vector.

$$\therefore \qquad \dot{\mathbf{r}} = 2t\mathbf{i} + 3t^2\mathbf{j} \Rightarrow \mathbf{r} = t^2\mathbf{i} + t^3\mathbf{j} + c$$

(Don't forget the + c when integrating. In this case c is a constant *vector*.)

But when $t = 0$, $\mathbf{r} = \mathbf{i} + 4\mathbf{j}$ $\therefore$ $c = \mathbf{i} + 4\mathbf{j}$

$$\Rightarrow \mathbf{r} = t^2\mathbf{i} + t^3\mathbf{j} + \mathbf{i} + 4\mathbf{j}$$

$$\Rightarrow \mathbf{r} = (t^2 + 1)\mathbf{i} + (t^3 + 4)\mathbf{j}, \text{ the required position vector.}$$

The previous ten examples should have given you an idea of the variety of ways vector methods can be used in mechanics. Now it's your turn. Work carefully through Exercises 1 to 24 on pp. 118–120.

Addition of vectors

If Jon is walking along at 1 m s^{-1} and then walks on to a moving walkway which itself is moving at 1.5 m s^{-1}, his speed will increase to $1 + 1.5 = 2.5$ m s^{-1}.

Figure 8.7

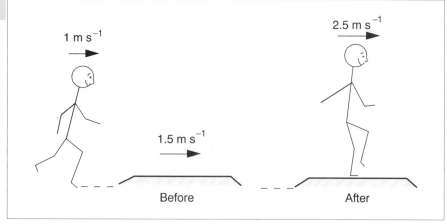

This provides an example where we *add* velocities.

Example   A plane with an airspeed of $(7\mathbf{i} + 6\mathbf{j})$ m s^{-1} has its speed increased by wind of $(-\mathbf{i} + 2\mathbf{j})$ m s^{-1}. What is the magnitude and direction of the plane's speed now?

Solution   Add the separate velocity vectors to get:

$$(7\mathbf{i} + 6\mathbf{j}) + (-\mathbf{i} + 2\mathbf{j}) = (6\mathbf{i} + 8\mathbf{j}) \text{ m s}^{-1}$$

Figure 8.8

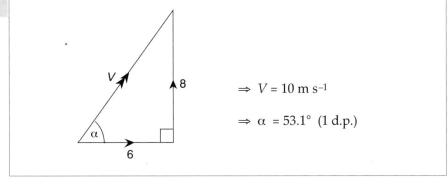

$\Rightarrow V = 10$ m s^{-1}

$\Rightarrow \alpha = 53.1°$ (1 d.p.)

∴   The actual speed of the plane is now 10 m s^{-1} on a bearing 036.9°.

Relative velocities

If Simon is running at 2 m s^{-1} and Annabel is running in the same direction at 3 m s^{-1}, then Annabel's speed relative to Simon's is $3 - 2 = 1$ m s^{-1}.

Figure 8.9

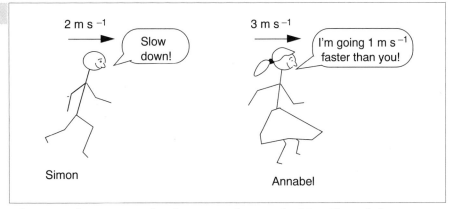

This provides an example where we *subtract* velocities. The rule is:

Velocity of A relative to Y = Velocity of A − Velocity of Y

Example	Particle A is moving with velocity vector $(5\mathbf{i} - 6\mathbf{j})$ m s^{-1}. Particle B is moving with velocity vector $(7\mathbf{i} + 2\mathbf{j})$ m s^{-1}. What is the velocity vector of B relative to A?

Solution	Velocity vector of B relative to A

$$= B's \text{ velocity vector} - A's \text{ velocity vector}$$
$$= (7\mathbf{i} + 2\mathbf{j}) - (5\mathbf{i} - 6\mathbf{j})$$
$$= (2\mathbf{i} + 8\mathbf{j}) \text{ m s}^{-1}$$

Relative velocities are covered in detail in Module M4.

You should now be able to answer Exercises 25 to 27 on pp. 120–121.

Practice questions

When you feel confident about the topics covered in this section, work through Exercises 28 to 31 on p. 121. They will give you a chance to revise the work covered so far.

EXERCISES

1 A force is given by the vector $(6\mathbf{i} + 8\mathbf{j})$ N. What is its magnitude and direction?

2 A force $(6\mathbf{i} + 9\mathbf{j})$ N acts on a particle of mass 3 kg. Find its acceleration vector. What is the magnitude of this acceleration?

3 The force $[(a - 8)\mathbf{i} + 6\mathbf{j}]$ N moves a particle parallel to the y-axis. Find the value of a.

4 The force $[8\mathbf{i} + (b + 10)\mathbf{j}]$ N moves a particle parallel to the x-axis. Find the value of b.

5 The force $[(a + 4)\mathbf{i} + (2a - 6)\mathbf{j}]$ N moves a particle parallel to the line $y = x$. Find the value of a.

6 Forces of $(3\mathbf{i} + 2\mathbf{j})$ N, $(4\mathbf{i} + 6\mathbf{j})$ N and $(-2\mathbf{i} + 4\mathbf{j})$ N act on a particle of mass 5 kg. Find its acceleration vector.

7 Forces (in newtons) of $4\mathbf{i} + \mathbf{j}$, $p\mathbf{i} + 3\mathbf{j}$ and $6\mathbf{i} + q\mathbf{j}$ act on a particle of mass 4 kg and produce an acceleration vector (in m s^{-2}) of $8\mathbf{i} + 12\mathbf{j}$. Find the values of p and q.

8 Forces (in newtons) of $4\mathbf{i} + 2\mathbf{j}$, $-2\mathbf{i} + \mathbf{j}$ and $3\mathbf{i} + 5\mathbf{j}$ act on a particle of mass 10 kg.

(a) What is its acceleration vector?

What is the smallest additional force that will move the particle:

(b) parallel to the y-axis

(c) parallel to the x-axis?

9 A mass has acceleration 10 m s^{-2} in the direction $4\mathbf{i} + 3\mathbf{j}$. What is its acceleration vector?

10 A mass has velocity 6.5 m s^{-1} in the direction $-5\mathbf{i} + 12\mathbf{j}$. What is its velocity vector?

11 An impulse has magnitude 20 Ns with direction vector $3\mathbf{i} - 4\mathbf{j}$. Express this impulse as a vector.

12 A force has magnitude 12.5 N and acts in the direction $7\mathbf{i} + 24\mathbf{j}$. Express this force as a vector.

13 A 3 kg mass is acted on by forces (in newtons) $3\mathbf{i} + a\mathbf{j}$, $b\mathbf{i} - 5\mathbf{j}$ and $7\mathbf{i} + 7\mathbf{j}$. The mass has acceleration vector (in m s^{-2}) $3\mathbf{i} + 4\mathbf{j}$.

(a) Find a and b.

(b) After 3 seconds the velocity vector of the mass (in m s^{-1}) is $20(\mathbf{i} + \mathbf{j})$. What was the initial velocity?

14 Initially a particle has a position vector (in m) of $\mathbf{i} + \mathbf{j}$ with a velocity vector (in m s^{-1}) of $4\mathbf{i} + 10\mathbf{j}$.

Its acceleration vector (in m s^{-2}) is constant and is given by $5\mathbf{i} - 2\mathbf{j}$. In its subsequent motion, what is its greatest distance parallel to the positive y-axis and when does this occur?

15 A 4 kg mass has velocity vector (in m s^{-1}) of $3\mathbf{i} + 4\mathbf{j}$.

(a) What is its kinetic energy?

(b) What is its momentum?

16 A 2 kg mass with velocity vector $(1.5\mathbf{i} + 8\mathbf{j})$ m s^{-1} hits a 5 kg mass with velocity vector $(-2\mathbf{i} + 8\mathbf{j})$ m s^{-1}.

They coalesce and move off together. Find:

(a) their common velocity after impact

(b) the total loss of kinetic energy

(c) the impulse received by the smaller mass.

17 A 90 kg missile moves with velocity (200**i** + 100**j**) m s^{-1}.

    (a) An explosion sends 50 kg off with velocity (250**i** + 50**j**) m s^{-1} and 40 kg off with velocity (100**i** + 200**j**) m s^{-1}. By considering momentum, explain why this couldn't have been caused by an internal explosion.

    (b) In fact, the explosion was caused by another missile of 15 kg hitting the 90 kg missile. If the 15 kg missile was brought to rest by the impact, find the velocity of the missile just before impact.

18 A particle at time t seconds has position vector **r** m given by **r** = $3t^2$**i** + $(4t - 6)$**j**. Find its velocity and acceleration at time $t = 4$.

19 A particle at time t seconds has acceleration vector (in m s^{-2}) given by **a** = 2**i** − **j**. Initially the particle is at rest at the point where position vector (in m) is 3**i** + **j**. Find the position vector of the particle at time t.

20 A particle at time t seconds has velocity vector (in m s^{-1}) given by **v** = $3t^2$**i** + $(t - 1)$**j**. Initially the particle was at the origin. Find its acceleration vector and position vector when $t = 3$.

21 The position vector **r** m of a mass m at time t seconds is given by **r** = $(3t^2 + 7)$**i** + $(3 + 5t)$**j**.

    Prove that the particle is moving under the action of a constant force and find it.

22 A particle of mass 2 kg moves under the action of a force (in newtons) 2**i** − 6**j**. Initially the particle is at the point whose position vector (in m) is **i** + **j** with a velocity vector (in m s^{-1}) **i** − **j**. Find the position vector of the particle at any time t.

23 A particle is acted upon by two forces $(2\mathbf{i} - t\mathbf{j})$ N and $(\mathbf{i} + 4t\mathbf{j})$ N at time t seconds. The particle is initially at rest. Find the momentum of the particle 5 seconds later.

24 The position vector **r** cm of a particle at time t seconds is given by

$$\mathbf{r} = 3(t - 1)\mathbf{i} + 4(3 - t)\mathbf{j}$$

    (a) Using graph paper, draw the path of the particle for $0 \le t \le 4$.

    (b) For what value of t is the particle closest to the origin?

    (c) Using (b), calculate the least distance of the particle from the origin.

25 An aircraft with an airspeed of $(5\mathbf{i} - 3\mathbf{j})$ m s^{-1} meets a wind of 7**j** m s^{-1}. What is the magnitude and direction of the aircraft's ground speed?

26 Particle R moves with velocity vector 3**i** m s^{-1} and particle S moves with velocity vector $(\mathbf{i} + 6\mathbf{j})$ m s^{-1}. What is the velocity vector of R relative to S?

27 Particle A is moving so that at time t seconds its position vector (in m) is given by $t\mathbf{i} + 3t\mathbf{j}$. Particle B is stationary at the point whose position vector is $2\mathbf{i} + \mathbf{j}$.

(a)   What is the position vector of A relative to B?

(b)   For what value of t is A nearest to B?

(c)   What is the shortest distance between A and B?

28 A particle P moves so that, at time t seconds, its position vector, $\mathbf{r}$ m, relative to a fixed origin, is given by $\mathbf{r} = (t^2 - 4t)\mathbf{i} + (t^3 + ft^2)\mathbf{j}$, $t > 0$,

where f is a constant.

(a)   Find an expression for the velocity of P at time t.

Given that the particle comes to instantaneous rest,

(b)   find the value of f.

29 A particle A, of mass 0.2 kg, has a velocity $(16\mathbf{i} - 12\mathbf{j})$ m s^{-1} and collides directly with another particle B, of mass 0.3 kg. Before the collision B is at rest. After the collision B has speed 10 m s^{-1}. Find:

(a)   the unit vector in the direction in which B begins to move

(b)   the velocities, in m s^{-1}, of A and B after the collision

(c)   the impulse, in Ns, received by A as a result of the collision.

30 A particle P moves so that at time t seconds its position vector $\mathbf{r}$ metres, relative to a final origin O, is given by:

$$\mathbf{r} = (2t - 3t^2 - 1)\ \mathbf{i} + (2t^2 - 2)\ \mathbf{j}$$

(a)   Find the velocity of P when $t = 2$

(b)   Hence find the speed of P when $t = 2$.

31 (In this question the velocities given are relative to the earth. The unit vectors $\mathbf{i}$ and $\mathbf{j}$ are directed due east and due north respectively.)

At time $t = 0$, two ice skaters P and Q have position vectors $2\mathbf{j}$ metres and $2\sqrt{3}\ \mathbf{i}$ metres respectively, relative to an origin O at the centre of the rink. The velocity of P is constant and equal to $3\mathbf{j}$ m/s and the velocity of Q is constant and equal to $\mathbf{v}$ m/s. Skater Q moves in a straight line and at time $t = T$ seconds collides with P.

(a)   Give a reason why $-2\sqrt{3}\ \mathbf{i} + 2\mathbf{j}$ is a vector in the direction of the velocity of Q relative to P.

(b)   Show that $\mathbf{v} = -k\sqrt{3}\ \mathbf{i} + (k + 3)\mathbf{j}$ when k is a positive constant.

Given that the speed of Q is $3\sqrt{3}$ m/s,

(c)   Find the value of k.

(d)   Find the value of T.

SUMMARY   You should now be able to:

- find the magnitude of any vector

e.g. $\mathbf{v} = 3\mathbf{i} + 4\mathbf{j} \Rightarrow$ 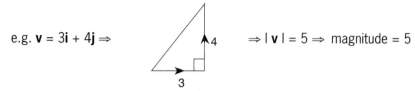 $\Rightarrow |\mathbf{v}| = 5 \Rightarrow$ magnitude = 5

- quote that the magnitude of a velocity vector is called the speed
- use the vector formulae $\mathbf{F} = m\mathbf{a}$,

  momentum $= m\mathbf{v}$, **Impulse** $= m\mathbf{v} - m\mathbf{u}$
- use $\mathbf{r}$ to represent a position vector (so that $\dot{\mathbf{r}}$ is the velocity vector and $\ddot{\mathbf{r}}$ the acceleration vector)
- integrate an acceleration vector to get the velocity vector (not forgetting +$\mathbf{c}$)
- integrate a velocity vector to get the position vector (not forgetting + $\mathbf{c}$)
- quote, and be able to use, the formula:

  Velocity vector of A relative to B = A's velocity vector – B's velocity vector.

9

Energy, work and power

INTRODUCTION In Section 7 we saw that kinetic energy is lost during a collision. If a situation occurs where kinetic energy is gained then work is done and the rate at which this work is done is called power. We shall be looking at these ideas in this section.

When you've finished this section you should both know, and be able to use, the definitions of:

- work done
- potential energy
- power.

Work done by a force

One of the four constant acceleration equations you met in Section 2 gives us:

$$v^2 = u^2 + 2as \implies \frac{1}{2}v^2 - \frac{1}{2}u^2 = as$$

Multiplying through by m and then using $F = ma$, this gives us:

$$\frac{1}{2}mv^2 - \frac{1}{2}mu^2 = Fs.$$

But the left-hand side of this equation is the gain in kinetic energy – you should remember this from Section 7.

$\therefore$ Gain in K.E. = Force × distance

But force × distance is defined as the work done by the force:

Gain in K.E. = Force × distance = Work done by force

It follows that the units of work done are joules (J).

Example	A 1500 kg car starts from rest and reaches a speed of 20 m s^{-1} after travelling 300 m. Neglecting resistances, find the constant driving force.

Solution	Gain in K.E. $= \frac{1}{2} \times 1500 \times 20^2 = 300\ 000$ J

Since distance covered is 300 m,

Force $\times$ 300 $= 300\ 000 \Rightarrow F = 1000$

(An alternative method would be to use $v^2 = u^2 + 2as$ to find the acceleration a [you get $\frac{2}{3}$ m s^{-2}] and then say $F = ma$.

Use this method if you prefer.)

This constant driving force of the car is called its *tractive force*.

$\therefore$ The car has a tractive force of 1000 N.

Example	A body of mass 20 kg has velocity 20 m s^{-1} at the foot of a rough plane inclined at 30° to the horizontal, and 2 m s^{-1} when it has travelled 40 m up the plane. Find the constant frictional force exerted by the plane on the body.

Solution	Loss in K.E. $= \frac{1}{2} \times 20 \times 20^2 - \frac{1}{2} \times 20 \times 2^2 = 3960$

Component of weight down the plane

$$= 20 \times 9.8 \times \sin 30° = 98 \text{ N.}$$

(See Exercise 4 of Section 4 if you need a refresher course here.)

If the frictional force down the plane is F, then:

$(F + 98) \times 40 = 3960 \Rightarrow F = 1$

$\therefore$ The frictional force exerted by the plane $= 1$ N

You should now be able to answer Exercises 1 to 4 on page 129.

Potential energy

Imagine a particle of mass m falling freely through the air. Suppose that at heights h_1 and h_2 its downward speeds are v_1 and v_2 respectively.

Figure 9.1

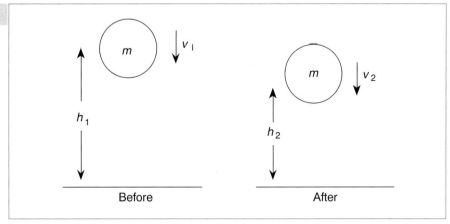

Before   After

The force acting on the mass is mg and the distance covered is $h_1 - h_2$

∴   Using the rule work done = gain in K.E. we get:

$$mg(h_1 - h_2) = \frac{1}{2}mv_2^2 - \frac{1}{2}mv_1^2$$

This rearranges to give:

$$\frac{1}{2}mv_1^2 + mg\,h_1 = \frac{1}{2}mv_2^2 + mg\,h_2$$

The quantities $mg\,h_1$ and $mg\,h_2$ are called *potential energy* (or P.E. for short).

∴ In this case K.E. + P.E. gives the same answer both before and after, *in this case K.E. + P.E. is a constant*. This is known as the principle of conservation of energy.

It can be proved that if a particle goes down a smooth slope or any smooth curve, then K.E. + P.E. remains constant. The crucial thing to remember is that *it must be smooth* and that the only forces acting are the weight and normal reaction to it.

Example	A particle of mass 6 kg is 8 m above a fixed horizontal surface. Taking that surface as having zero potential energy, find the potential energy of the particle.

Solution

Figure 9.2

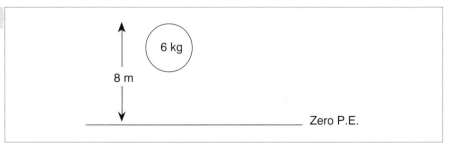

P.E. of particle $= mgh = 6 \times 9.8 \times 8 = 470.4$ J

Two things to notice here. Firstly, you need a line of reference (zero P.E.) before you can start talking about potential energy. Secondly, the units of P.E. are joules.

Example	A smooth length of tube has the strange shape shown below. It is held in a vertical plane and a marble of mass 10 grammes is released into the tube at the opening A. With what speed does the marble appear again at B?

Figure 9.3

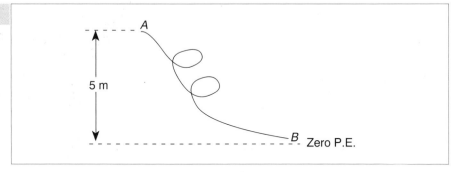

Solution   The tube is smooth $\therefore$ we can use the rule K.E. + P.E. = constant.

$$\therefore \qquad \frac{1}{2} \times 0.01 \times 0^2 + 0.01 \times 9.8 \times 5 = \frac{1}{2} \times 0.01 \times v^2 + 0$$

(I've taken the lower level as having zero P.E.)

$$\Rightarrow 0.49 = 0.005v^2 \Rightarrow v = 9.9 \quad (1 \text{ d.p.})$$

$\therefore \qquad$ The marble appears with a speed of 9.9 m s^{-1}

(If you go on to study Module M2, then you'll meet this idea again when tackling circular motion.)

You should now be able to answer Exercises 5 to 7 on pp. 129–130.

Power

Power is the rate at which work is done.

Now work $W = Fs$, where the force F is constant.

$$\therefore \quad \text{Power} = \frac{dW}{dt} = \frac{d}{dt}(Fs) = F\frac{ds}{dt} = Fv \quad \text{(where } F \text{ is a } \textit{constant} \text{ force)}$$

> Power = force × velocity (for constant force)

and the units of power are watts, written W.

Example   Find the power necessary for a train of mass 4×10^5 kg to travel at 80 km h^{-1} against resistance of 60 N per 10^3 kg.

Solution   Resisting force = 400 × 60 = 24 000 N

Travelling at constant speed ∴ tractive force of the engine is also 24 000 N

80 km h^{-1} = $\frac{80}{18} \times 5 = 22\frac{2}{9}$ m s^{-1} (see the Summary of Section 2 if you've forgotten that technique.)

$$\therefore \quad \text{Power} = 24\,000 \times 22\tfrac{2}{9} = 533\,000 \text{ W (3 s.f.)} = 533 \text{ kW}$$

Example   A train of mass 500 000 kg is travelling at 30 m s^{-1} up a slope of 1 in 100. The frictional resistance is 50 N per 1000 kg. Find the rate at which the engine is working.

Solution   Component of weight down the plane

$$= 500\,000 \times 9.8 \times \frac{1}{100} = 49\,000 \text{ N}$$

$\left(\text{See Exercise 4 in Section 4 if necessary. Also}\right.$

'a slope of 1 in 100' $\Rightarrow = \sin \theta = \frac{1}{100}\Big)$

Frictional force down plane = 500 × 50   = 25 000 N

∴ Tractive force of the engine   = 74 000 N

∴ Rate of working = power = 74 000 × 30 = 2220 kW

Example The total mass of an engine train is 2×10^5 kg and the total resistances to motion amount to $\frac{1}{200}$ of the total weight. What is the power of the engine if it can just keep the train moving at a uniform speed of 108 km h^{-1} on the level?

Solution Total resistance to motion $= \frac{1}{200} \times 2 \times 10^5 \times 9.8$ N $= 9800$ N.

The speed is uniform $\therefore$ the tractive force of the engine must also equal 9800 N.

The speed is 108 km h^{-1} = $108 \times \frac{5}{18}$ m s^{-1} = 30 m s^{-1}

$\therefore$ Power = $9800 \times 30 = 294\,000$ W

$\therefore$ The power of the engine is 294 kW.

Example An engine of 245 kW is taking a train of mass 2×10^5 kg up an incline of 1 in 250, and the resistance equals 3000 N. What is the maximum uniform speed of the train in km h^{-1}?

Solution Component of weight down the slope $= 2 \times 10^5 \times 9.8 \times \frac{1}{250}$ N $= 7840$ N

$\therefore$ Total resistance to motion = (7840 + 3000) N =10 840 N

The speed is uniform $\therefore$ the tractive force of the engine must also equal 10 840 N.

$\therefore$ Power = 245 kW $\Rightarrow$ 245 000 = 10840v, where v is the uniform speed

$\therefore$ $v = 22.60$ m s^{-1} or $22.60 \times \frac{18}{5} = 81.4$ km h^{-1}

$\therefore$ The maximum uniform speed is 81.4 km h^{-1}.

You should now be able to answer Exercises 8 to 13 on pp. 130–131.

Practice questions

When you feel confident about the topics covered in this section, work through Exercises 14 to 18 on pp. 131–132. They will give you a chance to revise the work covered so far and to practise more 'A' level exam-type questions.

EXERCISES

1 Assuming the mass of 1 m³ of water is 1000 kg, find the work done in giving 1 m³ of water a velocity of 8 m s⁻¹.

2 Find the work done in raising a body of mass 50 kg a distance of 8 m into a space craft stationary on the surface of the moon. (Take the moon's gravity to be 1.65 m s⁻².)

3 A boy of mass 40 kg slides down a rough chute inclined at 60° to the horizontal. If the boy starts from rest and if there is a constant frictional resistance of 60 N, with what velocity will he pass the point 10 m from his starting point?

4 A bullet of mass 10 grammes, velocity 600 m s⁻¹, enters 2.4 m into the protective sandbags before coming to rest. What is the resisting force of the sandbags (assumed constant)?

5 A body of mass 20 kg slides down a smooth plane inclined at 30° to the horizontal. Initially it is at rest. What is its speed when it has travelled 5 m down the plane?

6 A smooth particle of mass 0.02 kg is thrown into the tubular contraption shown below with an initial speed of 3 m s⁻¹. With what speed does it come flying out of the hole *H*?

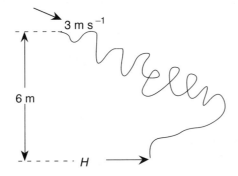

3 m s⁻¹

6 m

H

(Assume that the smooth tube is one continuous length and that it is held in a vertical plane.)

7 A disused and damaged (but smooth) fairground switchback has a vertical cross-section as shown below:

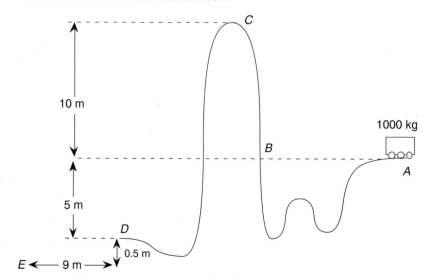

The switchback is continuous from A to D but there is a 0.5 m drop and a 9 m gap from D to E. A 1000 kg car is stationary at A.

(a) The car slips down on to the switchback. What happens?

(b) If instead the car has an initial velocity of 6 m s^{-1}, what happens now?

(c) What happens to the car if its initial velocity is 15 m s^{-1}?

8 A crane raises a 5000 kg steel girder at 0.4 m s^{-1}. Assuming that work is not lost in driving the crane, what is the power of the crane's engine?

9 A machine for firing clay pigeons throws 3 'birds' a minute. The mass of each 'bird' is 0.08 kg and the velocity with which each leaves the machine is 20 m s^{-1}. Find the power necessary to drive the machine assuming half of it is lost in the machine.

10 Find the kW used by a fire pump which raises water a distance of 4 m and delivers 0.12 m^3 a minute at a speed of 10 m s^{-1}. (Assume that 1 m^3 of water weighs 1000 kg.)

11 A car mass 800 kg ascends a hill of 1 in 10 at 20 m s^{-1}, the air resistance being 200 N. What power is the engine producing?

12 A light motorcycle whose mass including rider is 200 kg can go at 10 m s^{-1} up a plane of inclination θ, where sin $\theta = \dfrac{1}{14}$ and at 20 m s^{-1} down the same plane. If the resistance varies as the square of the speed and the power developed by the machine is constant, find the power developed.

13 The engine of a 5000 kg coach can work at 40 kW. If the resistance to motion is 1500 N, find the maximum speed along the level and up a slope of angle θ, where $\sin \theta = \dfrac{1}{98}$.

14 A car of mass 900 kg pulls a trailer of mass 350 kg along a straight level road against a total resistance of 1250 N. Given that the car is using its full power of 45 kW, show that its acceleration is 1.4 m s⁻² when its speed is 54 km h⁻¹.

Find also the tension in the coupling between the car and the trailer at this speed, assuming that the total resistance is divided between the car and the trailer in the ratio of their masses.

15 A locomotive working at the rate of 240 kW pulls a train of total mass 56 000 kg (including the locomotive) up a straight track inclined to the horizontal at an angle θ, where $\sin \theta = \dfrac{1}{50}$. When the speed is 5 m s⁻¹, the acceleration is $\frac{1}{4}$ m s⁻². Find the total resistance at this speed.

16 A boy and his bicycle have a total mass of 60 kg. When he is working at a rate of 400 W his maximum speed on a level road is 5 m/s. Calculate the frictional resistance.

The boy ascends a slope inclined at an angle α to the horizontal where $\sin \alpha = \frac{1}{12}$. His work rate remains the same but the frictional resistance is now 110 N. Calculate his maximum speed up the slope.

The bicycle will overturn if its speed drops below 2 m/s. Calculate the angle of the steepest slope the boy can ascend, assuming that the frictional resistance is still 110 N, and his work rate is still the same.

17 A car of mass 560 kg is pulling a caravan of mass 240 kg along a horizontal road. There are constant resistances of 120 N to the motion of the car and 80 N to the motion of the caravan.

Given that the tractive force of the car is 1200 N, calculate:

(a)   the acceleration of the car and caravan

(b)   the tension in the tow-bar

(c)   the power of the car's engine when the speed is 12 m s⁻¹.

The car now pulls the caravan up a road inclined at θ to the horizontal, where $\sin \theta = \dfrac{1}{16}$. Assuming that the tractive force and the resistances are unchanged:

(d)   calculate the acceleration of the car and caravan

(e)   show that the tension in the tow-bar is unchanged.

18 The magnitude of the resistance to the motion of a motor coach is K newtons per tonne, where K is a constant. The motor coach has mass $4\frac{1}{2}$ tonnes. When travelling on a straight horizontal road with the engine working at 39.6 kW, the coach maintains a steady speed of 40 m/s.

(a) Show that $K = 220$

The motor coach ascends a straight road, which is inclined at an angle α to the horizontal, where $\sin \alpha = 0.3$ with the same power output and against the same constant resisting forces.

(b) Find, in joules to 2 s.f., the kinetic energy of the motor coach when it is travelling at its maximum speed up the slope.

SUMMARY

You should now know that:

- work done = force × distance (where the force is constant)
- the units of work done are J (joules)
- work done = gain in K.E.

  $\therefore Fs = \frac{1}{2}mv^2 - \frac{1}{2}mu^2$

- potential energy is mgh, when h is measured from some agreed level
- on smooth surfaces there is a conservation of total energy

  $\therefore \frac{1}{2}mv_1^2 + mg\,h_1 = \frac{1}{2}mv_2^2 + mg\,h_2$

- the units of P.E. are J (joules)
- power is the rate of doing work
- the units of power are W (watts)
- power = force × velocity (where the force is constant)
- the driving force of an engine is known as its tractive force.

Solutions

Section 1

1 (a) $\mathbf{i} + 3\mathbf{j}$ (b) $-2\mathbf{i}$ (c) $3\mathbf{i} - 2\mathbf{j}$

    (d) $-2\mathbf{i} + 5\mathbf{j}$ (e) $2\mathbf{i} - 5\mathbf{j}$

2 From A to B you go 3 along the x-axis and 7 up the y-axis

$$\therefore \; \overrightarrow{AB} = \begin{pmatrix} 3 \\ 7 \end{pmatrix} \text{ or } \overrightarrow{AB} = 3\mathbf{i} + 7\mathbf{j}$$

Also $\overrightarrow{BA} = \begin{pmatrix} -3 \\ -7 \end{pmatrix}$ or $\overrightarrow{BA} = -3\mathbf{i} - 7\mathbf{j}$

(Questions 1(e) and 2 have illustrated the following useful general rule: $\overrightarrow{PQ} = -\overrightarrow{QP}$).

3

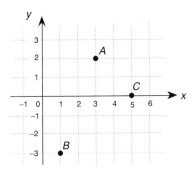

Beginning at B, if you go 4 along the x-axis and 3 up the y-axis, you finish up at C

$\therefore C$ has coordinates (5,0).

4 D has coordinates (3,2). E has coordinates (7,10)

$$\therefore \; \overrightarrow{DE} = \begin{pmatrix} 4 \\ 8 \end{pmatrix}.$$

5 (a) $\overrightarrow{PQ} = \begin{pmatrix} 2 \\ 5 \end{pmatrix}$ (b) $|\overrightarrow{PQ}| = \sqrt{29}$

6 $\overrightarrow{PQ} = \begin{pmatrix} 2 \\ 6 \end{pmatrix} \Rightarrow |\overrightarrow{PQ}| = \sqrt{40}$

7 $\mathbf{a} + \mathbf{b} = \begin{pmatrix} 4 \\ 2 \end{pmatrix} \Rightarrow |\mathbf{a} + \mathbf{b}| = \sqrt{20}$

8 (a) rigid body or particle
    (b) lamina
    (c) uniform rod or light rod
    (d) rigid body or particle
    (e) inextensible string
    (f) extensible string
    (g) particle attached to a rod (possibly uniform)
    (h) a particle or solid sphere
    (i) uniform rod or light rod
    (j) a particle flying through the air.

Section 2

1 (a) $\dfrac{30}{2}$ = 15 m s^{-1} (b) $\dfrac{-20}{2}$ = – 10 m s^{-1}
(c) 0. At rest

2 (a) Gradient = – 10 km in 5 min
∴ Velocity = –120 km h^{-1} & speed = 120 km h^{-1}

(b) 0. At rest

3 (a) $\dfrac{10}{4}$ = 2.5 m s^{-2} (b) Less acceleration
(c) 12 seconds (d) 2 seconds

(e) $\dfrac{4 \times 10}{2}$ + 4 × $\left(\dfrac{10 + 15}{2}\right)$ + 2 × 15 + $\dfrac{2 \times 15}{2}$

= 115 m

4 (a) $\dfrac{15}{1}$ = 15 m s^{-2} (b) $\dfrac{15}{2}$ = 7.5 m s^{-2}
(The acceleration is –7.5 m s^{-2} but the
deacceleration (or retardation) is 7.5 m s^{-2}.)
(c) 1 second (d) $\dfrac{2 \times 15}{2}$ = 15 m

(e) $\dfrac{1 \times 15}{2}$ + 3 × 15 + $\dfrac{2 \times 15}{2}$ = 67.5 m

5 (a) $\dfrac{2}{120}$ = $\dfrac{1}{60}$ m s^{-2} (b) 5 m s^{-1}

(c) $\dfrac{3}{120}$ = $\dfrac{1}{40}$ m s^{-2}

(d) 60 × 5 = 300 m. (e) 120 × $\left(\dfrac{5 + 2}{2}\right)$ = 420 m

6 36 km/h = 10 m/s

	u	v	a	s	t
∴	10	0		60	?

∴ $s = (\dfrac{u + v}{2})t$ ⇒ 60 = 5t ⇒ t = 12 seconds

7 48 km/h = 13$\dfrac{1}{3}$ m/s and 4 minutes = 240
seconds.

	u	v	a	s	t
∴	13$\frac{1}{3}$	0		?	240

∴ $s = (\dfrac{u + v}{2})t$ ⇒ s = 1600 m = 1.6 km

8

u	v	a	s	t
0	?	9·8	40	

∴ $v^2 = u^2 + 2as$ ⇒ v^2 = 0 + 2 × 9.8 × 40
⇒ v = 28 m s^{-1}

9

u	v	a	s	t
7	13	?		3

∴ $v = u + at$ ⇒ 13 = 7 + 3a ⇒ a = 2 m s^{-2}

10 60 km h^{-1} = 16$\dfrac{2}{3}$ m s^{-1} and 1 min = 60 secs.

	u	v	a	s	t
∴		16$\frac{2}{3}$	0.1	?	60

Find u first. ∴ $v = u + at$ ⇒ 16$\dfrac{2}{3}$ = u + 6
⇒ u = 10$\dfrac{2}{3}$

Now find s ∴ $s = (\dfrac{u + v}{2})t$

⇒ $s = (\dfrac{10\frac{2}{3} + 16\frac{2}{3}}{2})60$ ⇒ s = 820 m

11

u	v	a	s	t
12.5	0	?		100

∴ $v^2 = u^2 + 2as$ ⇒ 0 = 12.5^2 + 200a
⇒ a = – 0.78 m s^{-2} (2 d.p.)

∴ Retardation is + 0.78 m s^{-2}

12 (a)

u	v	a	s	t
30	0	–1.5	?	

∴ $v^2 = u^2 + 2as$ ⇒ 0 = 30^2 – 3s ⇒ s = 300 m

(b)

u	v	a	s	t
30	?	–1.5	273	

∴ $v^2 = u^2 + 2as$ ⇒ v^2 = 30^2 – 2 × 1.5 × 273
⇒ v = 9 m s^{-1}

13 (a)

u	v	a	s	t
14	34		?	20

∴ $s = (\dfrac{u + v}{2})t$ ⇒ s = 480 m

also $v = u + at$ ⇒ a = 1 m s^{-2} (Needed in (b)!)

(b)

u	v	a	s	t
14		1	240	?

∴ $s = ut + \dfrac{1}{2}at^2$ ⇒ 240 = 14t + 0.5t^2
⇒ t = 12 or –40
⇒ t = 12 seconds

14 After 5 seconds: $s = 2 \times 5 + \dfrac{1}{2}a5^2$
⇒ s = 10 + 12.5a … ①
After 6 seconds: $s + 13 = 2 \times 6 + \dfrac{1}{2}a6^2$
⇒ $s + 13$ = 12 + 18a … ②
Solve ① and ② simultaneously and
get a = 2 m s^{-2}

∴ $v = u + at$ ⇒ v = 2 + 2 × 6 = 14 m s^{-1}

15 ↓ :

u	v	a	s	t
0		9.8	?	2

∴ $s = ut + \dfrac{1}{2}at^2$ ⇒ s = 19.6m

16 $5 \div 2 = 2\frac{1}{2}$ seconds to reach the top

$\therefore \uparrow:$

u	v	a	s	t
0	–9.8	?		$2\frac{1}{2}$

Find u first $\therefore$ $v = u + at \Rightarrow u = 24.5$ m s^{-1}

Now find s $\therefore$ $s = \left(\dfrac{u + v}{2}\right)t \Rightarrow s = 30.625$ m

17 (a) $\uparrow:$

u	v	a	s	t
0	?	2		10

$\therefore$ $v = u + at \Rightarrow v = 20$ m s^{-1}

(b) Ballast has initial velocity of 20 m s^{-1} upwards and is pulled downwards by gravity.

$\therefore \downarrow:$

u	v	a	s	t
–20	?	9.8		10

(The initial velocity downwards is –20 m s^{-1}. A tricky point?)

$\therefore$ $v = u + at \Rightarrow v = 78$ m s^{-1}

18 $\uparrow:$

u	v	a	s	t
20	0	–9.8	?	

$\therefore$ $v^2 = u^2 + 2as \Rightarrow s = 20.4$ m (1 d.p.)

19 (a) $\downarrow:$

u	v	a	s	t
0	?	9.8	5	

$\therefore$ $v^2 = u^2 + 2as \Rightarrow v = 9.90$ m s^{-1} (2 d.p.)

$\therefore$ Rebounds with 4.95 m s^{-1}

(b) $\uparrow:$

u	v	a	s	t
4.95	0	–9.8		?

$\therefore$ $v^2 = u^2 + 2as \Rightarrow s = 1.25$ m

20

u	v	a	s	t
0	?	2g		10

$\therefore$ $v = u + at \Rightarrow v = 20g \Rightarrow v = 196$ m s^{-1} the additional velocity

21 Suppose they land after the first stone has been falling for t seconds.

$\therefore$ 1st stone:

u	v	a	s	t
0		9.8		t

and 2nd stone:

u	v	a	s	t
11		9.8		$t - 1$

They have the same s. Using $s = ut + \frac{1}{2}at^2$ twice we get $0 + 4.9t^2 = 11(t - 1) + 4.9(t - 1)^2$

$\Rightarrow t = \dfrac{6 \cdot 1}{1 \cdot 2} = 5.08$ seconds (2 d.p.)

$\therefore$ Height of cliff $= 4.9t^2 = 4.9 \times 5.08^2$

$= 127$ m (3 s.f.)

22 The velocity–time graph is shown below.

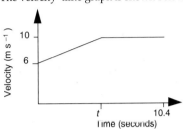

Distance $= 100$ m $\Rightarrow$ area $= 100$

$\Rightarrow t\left(\dfrac{6 + 10}{2}\right) + (10.4 - t)\,10 = 100$

$\Rightarrow t = 2$ seconds

$\therefore$ Acceleration $=$ gradient of 1st section

$= \dfrac{10 - 6}{2} = 2$ m s^{-2}

Distance $=$ area of 1st section

$= 2 \times \dfrac{6 \times 10}{2} = 16$ m

23 The velocity–time graph is shown below.

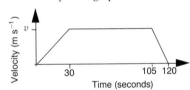

Distance $= 2145$ m $\Rightarrow$ area $= 2145$

$\Rightarrow 15v + 75v + \dfrac{15v}{2} = 2145$

$\Rightarrow v = 22$ m s^{-1}

Acceleration $=$ gradient $= \dfrac{22}{30} = 0.73$ms^{-2} (2 d.p.)

24 We get the following velocity–time graph:

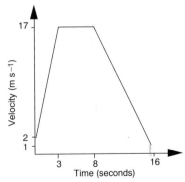

(Gradient of 1st section has to be 5 and we are told that the gradient of the last section is –2.)

(a) Constant velocity = 17 m s^{-1}

(b) Distance covered = area

$$= 3 \times \frac{19}{2} + 5 \times 17 + 8 \times \frac{18}{2} = 185.5 \text{ m}.$$

25 The velocity–time graph is shown below.

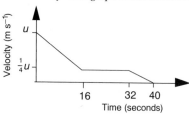

(a) (i) Gradient $= \dfrac{-\frac{3}{4}u}{16} = -\dfrac{3}{64}u$

∴ Retardation $= \dfrac{3}{64}u$ m s^{-2}

(ii) Gradient $= \dfrac{-\frac{1}{4}u}{8} = -\dfrac{1}{32}u$

∴ Retardation $= \dfrac{1}{32}u$ m s^{-2}

(b) 1st area $= 16 \times \left(\dfrac{u + \frac{1}{4}u}{2}\right) = 10u$

2nd area $= \dfrac{8 \times \frac{1}{4}u}{2} = u$

∴ Total area = 11u, as required

(c) Middle area $= 16 \times \dfrac{1}{4}u = 4u$

∴ Total distance = 15u = 45 $\Rightarrow$ u = 3

26

A:	u	v	a	s	t
	u		f		$t + 10$

and B:	u	v	a	s	t
	u		$2f$		t

Use $v = u + at$ and equate equal velocities.

∴ $u + f(t + 10) = u + 2ft$

$\Rightarrow t = 10 \Rightarrow$ A going for 20 seconds

∴ Common velocity at that time = $u + 20f$

∴ A:	u	v	a	s	t
	u	$u + 20f$	f		20

and B:	u	v	a	s	t
	u	$u + 20f$	$2f$		10

Now use $s = \left(\dfrac{u + v}{2}\right)t$ twice and get

A distance $= (u + 10f)20$ and

B distance $= (u + 10f)10$

∴ A distance = 2 × B distance

That was a hard question!

27

P:	u	v	a	s	t
	1		2		$t + 4$

Q:	u	v	a	s	t
	16		1		t

(Where t is measured from the time that Q starts.)

Using $s = ut + \frac{1}{2}at^2$ twice, Q's distance is greater than P's distance when

$$16t + \tfrac{1}{2}t^2 > 1(t + 4) + \tfrac{1}{2} \times 2 \times (t + 4)^2$$

This simplifies to $0 > t^2 - 14t + 40$

$\Rightarrow 0 > (t - 4)(t - 10)$

$\Rightarrow 4 < t < 10$

∴ Q overtakes P after 4 + 4 = 8 seconds and P overtakes Q after 4 + 10 = 14 seconds

After 8 seconds, common distance = 72 m

After 14 seconds, common distance = 210 m

Another tricky one – especially if you've forgotten how to solve inequalities.

28 (a)

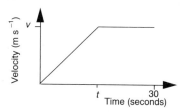

(b) Gradient of first section is 2.3

∴ $2.3 = \dfrac{v}{t}$ ∴ $v = 2.3\,t$

(c) Total area = 776.25

∴ $776.25 = \dfrac{vt}{2} + (30 - t)\,v$

∴ $776.25 = 30\,v - \dfrac{vt}{2}$

Now substitute for v from (b)

∴ $776.25 = 30 \times 2.3\,t - \dfrac{2.3t \times t}{2}$

∴ $1552.5 = 138t - 2.3\,t^2$

∴ $675 = 60t - t^2$, as required.

Section 3

1 (a) $a = 5$ m s^{-2}

(b) $\therefore$ u v a s $t \Rightarrow v = 20$ m s^{-1}

      0   ?   5   4

2 (a) $600 = 150a \Rightarrow a = 4$ m s^{-2} $\therefore$

(b) u v a s $t \Rightarrow v = 16$ m s^{-1}

    4   ?   4   3

3 (a) $F = 60$N   (b) $s = 40$ m

4 $P - 20 = 56 \Rightarrow P = 76$ N

5 (a) $a = 0$ (b) $F = 40$ N

6 (a) $a = 0$ (b) $P = 30$ N.

(c) Then $30 = -8a \Rightarrow a = -3.75$ m s^{-2}

    $\Rightarrow$ retardation $= 3.75$ m s^{-2}

7 (a) $F - 200 = 120 \Rightarrow F = 320$ N.

(b) Then $200 = -40a \Rightarrow a = -5$ m s^{-2}

    $\Rightarrow$ retardation $= 5$ m s^{-2}

8 $a = 2$ m s^{-2}

$\therefore$ u v a s $t \Rightarrow v = 12$ m s^{-1}

   0   ?   2   6

Then $a = -0.4$ m s^{-2}

$\therefore$ u v a s $t \Rightarrow t = 25$ seconds

   12   2 -0.4 ?

$\therefore$ Total time $= 6 + 25 = 31$ seconds

9 $a = 2$ m s^{-2}

$\therefore$ u v a s t $\Rightarrow v = 20$ m s^{-1}

   0   ?   2   ??   10 $\Rightarrow s = 100$ m

Then $a = -4$ m s^{-2}

$\therefore$ u v a s t $\Rightarrow t = 5$ seconds

   20   0 -4 ?   ?? $\Rightarrow s = 50$ m

$\therefore$ Total time $= 10 + 5 = 15$ seconds

$\therefore$ Total distance $= 100 + 50 = 150$ m

10 u v a s t

    5   0   ?   1.25 $\Rightarrow$ $a = -10$ m s^{-1}

Since 400 tonnes $= 400000$ kg,

$F = 400000 \times 10 = 4$ million N

11

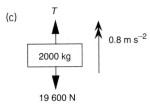

$3 \times 9.8 = 29.4$ N

$\therefore$ $29.4 - R = 3 \times 2$

$\therefore$ $R = 23.4$ N

12 (a)

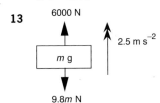

$19\,600$ N

$\therefore$ $19\,600 - T = 2000 \times 0.5$

$\therefore$ $T = 18\,600$ N

(b) No acceleration $\therefore$ $T = $ Weight $= 19\,600$ N

(c)

T

2000 kg   0.8 m s^{-2}

$19\,600$ N

$\therefore$ $T - 19\,600 = 2000 \times 0.8$

$\therefore$ $T = 21\,200$ N

13

6000 N

$m\,g$ 2.5 m s^{-2}

$9.8m$ N

$\therefore$ $6000 - 9.8m = m \times 2.5$

$\therefore$ $6000 = 12.3\,m$

$\therefore$ $m = 488$ kg (3 s.f.)

(6 kN is shorthand for 6 kilonewtons i.e. 6000 N)

14

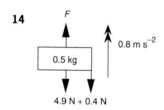

$\therefore F - 5.3 = 0.5 \times 0.8$

$\therefore F = 5.7$ N

15 (a)

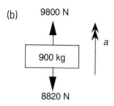

No acceleration $\therefore F = 9800$ N

(b)

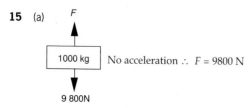

$\therefore 9800 - 8820 = 900a$

$\therefore a = 1.09$ m s^{-2} (2 d.p.)

16 Upwards thrust = weight = 5880 N.
(See question 15?)

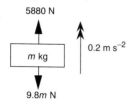

$\therefore 5880 - 9.8$ m = 0.2 m

$\therefore$ m = 588 $\therefore$ 12 kg thrown out

17 $50 - T = 15a$ $\therefore$ $a = 2$ m s^{-2}, $T = 20$ N
$T - 10 = 5a$

18 $63 - T = 25a$ $\therefore$ $a = 1.5$ m s^{-2}, $T = 25.5$ N
$T - 3 = 15a$

19 $395 - T = 100a$
$T - 3 - S = 20a$
$S - 2 = 10a$

Add all three equations to get $a = 3$ m s^{-2}
$\therefore$ $T = 95$ N, $S = 32$ N

20 $1960 - T = 200a$ $\therefore a = 7.84$ m s^{-2}, $T = 392$ N
$T = 50a$

21 $1960 - T = 200a$ $\therefore$ $a = 5.88$ m s^{-2} (2 d.p.)
$T - 20 = 130a$ $\therefore$ $T = 784$ N (3 s.f.)

22 $78.4 - T = 8a$ $\therefore$ $a = 5.88$ m s^{-2},
$T - 19.6 = 2a$ $T = 31.36$ N

23 $117.6 - T = 60$ $T - 9.8m = 5m$

Add these two equations to get
$117.6 - 9.8m = 60 + 5m$

$\Rightarrow 57.6 = 14.8 \, m$ $\Rightarrow m = 3.89$ kg (2 d.p.)

$\therefore T = 57.6$ N

24 (a) & (b) $196 - T = 20a$ $\therefore$ $a = 3.27$ m s^{-2} (2 d.p.)
$T - 98 = 10a$

$\therefore$ u v a s t $\Rightarrow v = 3.92$ m s^{-1}
 $\quad$ 0   ?   3.27 ?? 1.2 $\Rightarrow s = 1.176$ m

Then (free fall): $\downarrow$:
 $\quad$ u v a s t $\Rightarrow v = 12.84$ m s^{-1} (2 d.p.)
 $\quad$ 3.92 ? 9.8 7.624 ?? $\Rightarrow t = 0.92$ s (2 d.p.)

(c) : $\downarrow$: u v a s t
 $\quad\quad\quad$ *$-$3.92   9.8 9.976   ?

$\therefore$ $v = 14.52$ m s^{-1} $\therefore$ $t = 1.88$ seconds

$\therefore$ Extra time $= 1.88 - 0.91 = 0.97$ seconds

(*The clever trick is to regard the 10 kg mass
as initially going downwards with a velocity of
-3.92 m s^{-1} when the string breaks.)

25 (a)

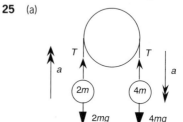

$4mg - T = 4ma$

$T - 2mg = 2ma$ $\therefore$ $a = \dfrac{1}{3}g$

(b) $T = 2\dfrac{2}{3}mg$

The string exerts the following forces on the pulley:

∴ force exerted by string on pulley = $2T$
$$= 5\tfrac{1}{3}\,mg$$

(Remember – the tensions at either end of a string are equal and opposite.)

26

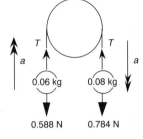

0.588 N   0.784 N

$0.784 - T = 0.08a$

$T - 0.588 = 0.06a$

∴ $a = 1.4\text{ms}^{-2}$, $T = 0.672$ N

27 (a)

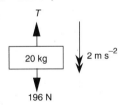

$196 - T = 20 \times 2 \quad \Rightarrow T = 156$ N

(b) No acceleration $\Rightarrow T = $ weight $= 294$ N

(c)

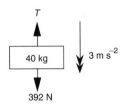

$T - 392 = 40 \times 3 \quad \Rightarrow T = 512$ N

Section 4

1

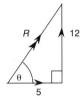

∴ $R = 13$ N   ∴ $\theta = 67.4°$ (1 d.p.)
∴ Bearing = 022.6° (1 d.p.)

2

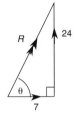

∴ $R = 25$ N   ∴ $\theta = 73.7°$ (1 d.p.)
∴ Bearing = 016.3° (1 d.p.)

3

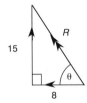

∴ $R = 17$ N   ∴ $\theta = 61.9°$ (1 d.p.)
∴ Bearing = 331.9° (1 d.p.)

4

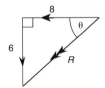

∴ $R = 10$ N   ∴ $\theta = 36.7°$ (1 d.p.)
∴ Bearing = 233.3° (1 d.p.)

5 (a)

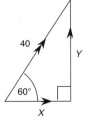

∴ $X = 40 \cos 60° = 20$ N
∴ $Y = 40 \sin 60° = 34.6$ N (1 d.p.)

(b)

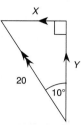

$\therefore$ $X = 20 \sin 10° = 3.5$ N (1 d.p.)
$\therefore$ $Y = 20 \cos 10° = 19.7$ N (1 d.p.)

(c)

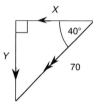

$\therefore$ $X = 70 \cos 40° = 53.6$ N (1 d.p.)
$\therefore$ $Y = 70 \sin 40° = 45.0$ N (1 d.p.)

(d)

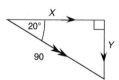

$\therefore$ $X = 90 \cos 20° = 84.6$ N (1 d.p.)
$\therefore$ $Y = 90 \sin 20° = 30.8$ N (1 d.p.)

6   (a)

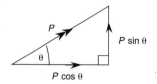

(b)

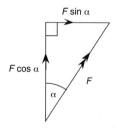

7

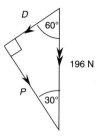

Weight = $20 \times 9.8 = 196$ N.

(a) $\therefore$ $D = 196 \sin 30° = 98$ N

(b) $\therefore$ $P = 196 \cos 30° = 170$ N (3 s.f.)

8

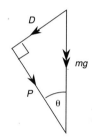

(a)   Component of weight down the plane
        = $mg \sin \theta$

(b)   Component of weight perpendicular
        to the plane = $mg \cos \theta$

You may have found questions 7 and 8 rather tricky.
I suggest that you learn by heart:

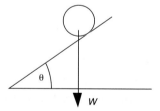

resolves to:

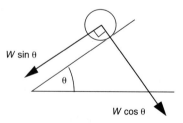

We'll be returning to this result again and again.

9 $(\rightarrow)$: $20 - 30 \cos 60° = 5$ N

$(\uparrow)$: $30 \sin 60° = 26$ N

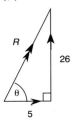

$\therefore$ $R = 26.5$ N (1 d.p.) and $\theta = 79°$ (2 s.f.)

$\therefore$ Bearing = 011° (2 s.f.)

10 $(\rightarrow)$: $70 - 40 \cos 30 = 35.4$ N

$(\uparrow)$: $50 - 40 \sin 30 = 30$ N

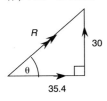

$\therefore$ $R = 46.5$ N (1 d.p.) and $\theta = 40°$ (2 s.f.)

$\therefore$ Bearing = 050° (2 s.f.)

11 $(\rightarrow)$: $40 + 50 \cos 20° - 70 \cos 40° = 33.36$ N

$(\uparrow)$: $30 - 70 \sin 40° + 50 \sin 20° = 2.11$ N

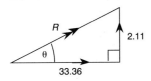

$\therefore$ $R = 33.4$ N (1 d.p.) and $\theta = 3.6°$ (1 d.p.)

$\therefore$ Bearing = 086.4° (1 d.p.)

12 $(\rightarrow)$: $10 + 30 \cos 60° - 20 \cos 60° = 15$ N

$(\uparrow)$: $30 \sin 60 + 20 \sin 60° - 5 = 38.3$ N

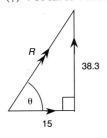

$\therefore$ $R = 41$ N (2 s.f.) and $\theta = 69°$ (2 s.f.)

$\therefore$ Bearing = 021° (2 s.f.)

13 $R = 8 \times 9.8 = 78.4$ N

14 $R = 78.4 + 10 \sin 30° = 83.4$ N

15 $R + 10 \sin 30° = 78.4 \Rightarrow R = 73.4$ N

16 $R = 78.4 \cos 30° \Rightarrow R = 67.9$ N (1 d.p.)

(If this causes trouble, refer back to Exercise 8.)

17 $R = 78.4 \cos 30° + 10 \sin 30°$

$\Rightarrow R = 72.9$ N (1 d.p.)

18 $R + 10 \sin 30° = 78.4 \cos 30°$

$\Rightarrow R = 62.9$ N (1 d.p.)

19

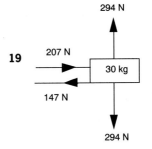

(a) Maximum frictional force
= $0.5 \times 294 = 147$ N.

$\therefore$ body moves.

$F = ma \Rightarrow 60 = 30a \Rightarrow$ acceleration = 2 m s^{-2}

(b) Maximum frictional force
= $0.4 \times 294 = 117.6$ N

$\therefore$ Body doesn't move.

20

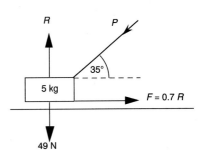

Steady velocity means no acceleration

$\therefore$ The forces balance in two directions.

$(\rightarrow)$: $P \cos 35° = 0.7R$ $\Big\}$

$(\uparrow)$: $R = 49 + P \sin 35°$

$\Rightarrow$ $P \cos 35° = 0.7(49 + P \sin 35°)$

$\Rightarrow$ $P = 82$ N (2 s.f.)

21

u	v	a	s	t
15	0		75	

$\Rightarrow a = -1.5 \text{ m s}^{-2}$

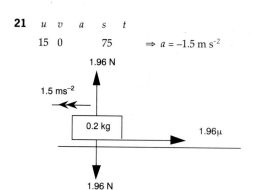

$F = ma$ ∴ $1.96\mu = 0.2 \times 1.5$ ∴ $\mu = 0.153$

22

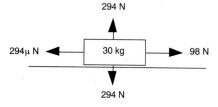

∴ $P = 148 + 207 = 355$ N

(Refer to Exercise 8 if you had trouble resolving the weight into 207 N and 444 N.)

23

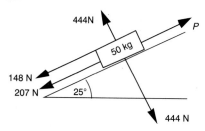

∴ $294\mu = 98$ ∴ $\mu = \frac{1}{3}$

(a)

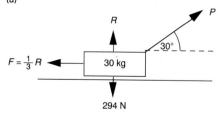

[Note that F is *against* the motion.]

$(\rightarrow) : P \cos 30° = \frac{1}{3}R$

$(\uparrow) : R + P \sin 30° = 294$

∴ $P = 95$ N (2 s.f.)

(b)

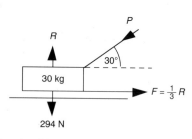

[Note that F is against the motion.]

$(\rightarrow) : P \cos 30° = \frac{1}{3}R$

$(\uparrow) : R = 294 + P \sin 30°$

∴ $P = 140$ N (3 s.f.)

24

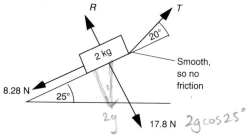

(If need be, refer to Exercise 8 for resolving the weight.)

Up plane: $T \cos 20° = 8.28$

Perpendicular to plane: $R + T \sin 20° = 17.8$

∴ $T = 8.8$ N (1 d.p.)

∴ $R = 14.8$ N (1 d.p.)

25 $24.5 - T = 2.5a$ $T - 49 = 10a$

∴ $a = -1.96 \text{ m s}^{-2}$ and so the 10 kg mass slides down the plane at 1.96 m s^{-2}.

∴ $T = 29.4$ N

26   Again, the 10 kg mass will slide *down* the plane.

$49 - (T + 1.73) = 10a$

$T - 24.5 = 2.5a$ ∴ $a = 1.82 \text{ ms}^{-2}$

27

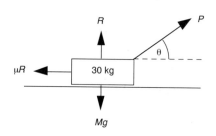

$(\rightarrow):\ P\cos\theta\ =\mu R$

$(\uparrow):\ R+P\sin\theta\ =Mg$

Eliminate R and get $P\cos\theta=\mu(Mg-P\sin\theta)$

$\Rightarrow P\cos\theta+\mu P\sin\theta\ =\mu Mg$

$\Rightarrow P=\dfrac{\mu Mg}{\cos\theta+\mu\sin}$

(An algebraic version of Exercise 23 (a).)

28

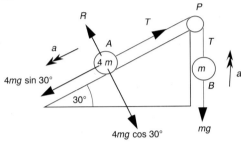

(a) $4mg\sin 30°-T=4ma$

$\Rightarrow 2mg-T\ =4ma$ and $T-mg=ma$

(b) Solve simultaneously to get

$a=\dfrac{1}{5}g$ and $T=1.2\,mg$

29

(a)

$\text{Tan }\theta=\dfrac{7}{24}\Rightarrow$

25 7   ... (*)
θ

Up plane: $T-Mg\sin\theta-\dfrac{11}{12}R=Ma$ ... ①

Perpendicular to plane: $R=Mg\cos\theta$ ... ②

Hanging mass: $2Mg-T=2Ma$ ... ③

Substitute for R in ①. Then add to ③

$\therefore 2Mg-Mg\sin\theta-\dfrac{11}{12}Mg\cos\theta=3Ma$

$\therefore 2Mg-Mg\times\dfrac{7}{25}-\dfrac{11}{2}Mg\times\dfrac{24}{25}=3Ma$

(from *)

$\therefore a=\dfrac{7}{25}g$, as required.

(b) $\downarrow:$ u v a s t

     0   ? $\dfrac{7}{25}g$ 25

$\therefore v^2=0^2+2\times\dfrac{7}{25}g\times 25$

$\therefore v=12\text{ m s}^{-1}$ (2 s.f.)

Section 5

1

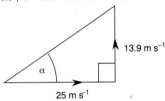

(a) $\uparrow:0=43.3-9.8t\Rightarrow t=4.42$ seconds

$\therefore$ time of flight $=2\times 4.42=8.84$ seconds

(b) $\rightarrow:$ range $=25\times 8.84=220.9$.m

(c) $\uparrow:s=\dfrac{43.3}{2}\times 4.42=95.7$ m

(d) $\uparrow:s=43.3\times 2-4.9\times 4=67$ m

(e) $\uparrow v=43.3-9.8\times 3\ =13.9$

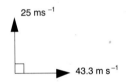

$\therefore\ \alpha=29°$ to horizontal

2

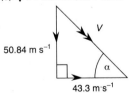

(a) $\uparrow:0=25-9.8t\ \therefore\ t=2.55$

$\therefore\ s=\dfrac{25}{2}\times 2.55=31.89$ m

$\therefore$ Greatest height $=131.89$ m.

(b) $\downarrow:131.89=4.9t^2\ \therefore\ t=5.188$ seconds

$\therefore$ Time of flight $=2.55+5.188=7.74$ seconds

(c) $\rightarrow:$ range $=43.3\times 7.74=335$ m

(d) $\downarrow v=9.8\times 5.188=50.84$

$\therefore\qquad v=66.8\text{ m s}^{-1}$

and $\alpha=49.6°$ to horizontal

3   (a) $\downarrow : 100 = 4.9t^2$ $\therefore\ 100 = 4.9t^2$
$\therefore\ t = 4.52$ seconds

(b) $\rightarrow$: range $= 60 \times 4.52 = 271$ m

(c) $\downarrow : s = 0 + \frac{1}{2} \times 9.8 \times 4 = 19.6$ m
$\therefore\ 80.4$ m above the sea

(d) $\downarrow\ v = 9.8 \times 3 = 29.4$

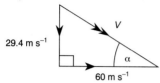

29.4 m s^{-1}

60 m s^{-1}

$\therefore\ \alpha = 26 \cdot 1°$ to horizontal

(e) $v = 66.82$ m s^{-1}

4   (a) $\uparrow : 15 = 20t - 4.9t^2$ $\therefore\ t = 0.99$ seconds or 3.09 (quadratic)

$\therefore$ Takes 0.99 seconds to reach P

(b) 3.09 seconds is the time to go up to Q and then fall back to P

$\therefore$ Time from P to $Q = \dfrac{3.09 - 0.99}{2} = 1.05$

seconds

(c) Time taken to reach Q is $0.99 + 1.05 = 2.04$ seconds

$\therefore\ \uparrow : s = \left(\dfrac{20 + 0}{2}\right) 2.04 = 20.4$ m.

$\therefore\ PQ = 20.4 - 15 = 5.4$ m

(d) $3.09 - 0.99 = 2.1$ seconds (see (b))

5 $\uparrow : 0 = 25 - 9.8t$ $\therefore\ t = 2.55$ seconds to reach maximum height

$\therefore$ Time of flight $= 2 \times 2.55 = 5.1$ seconds

$\rightarrow : s = 15 \times 5.1 = 76.5$ m

6   (a)

$\sin\theta = \dfrac{12}{13} \Rightarrow$

13   12 $\Rightarrow$ 13   12

5
(Pythagoras)

$\therefore\ u$ is the same as u $\dfrac{12}{13}u$

$\dfrac{5}{13}u$

$\rightarrow : 600 = \dfrac{5}{13} ut$ $\therefore\ ut = 1560$ $\therefore\ t = \dfrac{1560}{u}$

$\therefore$ Time to reach maximum height $= \dfrac{780}{u}$

$\uparrow : 0 = \dfrac{12}{13}u - 9.8 \times \dfrac{780}{u}$

$\Rightarrow\ 12u^2 = 99372 \Rightarrow u = 91$

(b) $\uparrow : s = \dfrac{1}{2}\left(\dfrac{12u}{13} + 0\right) \times \dfrac{780}{u} = 360$ m

(c) $\dfrac{1560}{u} = 17.1$ seconds

7

181.2 m s^{-1}

676.1 m s^{-1}

$\uparrow : 0 = 181.2 - 9.8t$ $\therefore\ t = 18.5$ seconds

$\therefore$ Time of flight $= 2 \times 18.5 = 37.0$ seconds

$\therefore\ \rightarrow :$ range $= 676.1 \times 37.0 = 25000$ m

8 $v = 12t^2 + 8,\ a = 24t$
$\therefore$ Velocity $= 56$ and acceleration $= 48$

9 $x = 2t^3 + 6t^2 + 4t,\ v = 6t^2 + 12t + 4,\ a = 12t + 12$
$\therefore$ Velocity $= 52$ and acceleration $= 36$

10 $v = 2t + 1 \Rightarrow v = 7$ m s^{-1}
$2t + 1 = 9 \Rightarrow t = 4$ seconds

11 $v = 4t^3 + c$ but $v = 6$ when $t = 1$ $\therefore\ v = 4t^3 + 2$
$\therefore\ t = 0 \Rightarrow v = 2$ m s^{-1}.
$4t^3 + 2 = 500 \Rightarrow t^3 = 124.5 \Rightarrow t = 4.99$ seconds

12 $\dfrac{dv}{dt} = 6t - t^2 = 0 \Rightarrow t = 0$ or 6

$x = t^3 - \dfrac{1}{12}t^4 + 9t + c$

$\therefore\ t = 0 \Rightarrow x = c$ and $t = 6 \Rightarrow x = 162 + c$

$\therefore$ Distance covered $= 162$ m

13 $v = 0$ when $t = 0$ or 1 minute
$v = \dfrac{4}{3}t - \dfrac{4}{3}t^2,\ x = \dfrac{2}{3}t^2 - \dfrac{4}{9}t^3$

(a) $t = 1 \Rightarrow x = \dfrac{2}{9}$

$\therefore$ Average velocity $= \dfrac{2}{9}$ km/min $= 13\dfrac{1}{3}$ km/h

(b) Maximum velocity when acceleration is zero

$\therefore \frac{4}{3} - \frac{8}{3}t = 0 \Rightarrow t = 0.5$ minute

$\Rightarrow v = \frac{1}{3}$ km/min = 20 km/h

14 (a) $x = t + 2t^2 + 2t^3 - 5$ (when $t = 1$, $x = 0$)

$\therefore t = 3 \Rightarrow x = 70$

$\Rightarrow$ average velocity $= \frac{70}{2} = 35$ m s^{-1}

(b) $t = 1$, $v = 11$ and $t = 3$, $v = 67$

$\Rightarrow$ average acceleration $= \frac{67 - 11}{2} = 28$ m s^{-2}

15 $v = kt - \frac{1}{12}t^2$ (when $t = 0$, $v = 0$)

$\therefore v = 60$, $t = 60 \Rightarrow 60 = 60k - 300 \Rightarrow k = 6$

$\therefore v = 6t - \frac{1}{12}t^2 \Rightarrow x = 3t^2 - \frac{1}{36}t^3$

(when $t = 0$, $x = 0$)

$\therefore t = 60 \Rightarrow x = 4800$ m

16 $v = 12t^2 - 4t^3$ ($v = 0$, $t = 0$),

$x = 4t^3 - t^4$ ($x = 0$, $t = 0$)

(a) $x = 0 \Rightarrow t = 4$ s $\Rightarrow v = -64$ m s^{-1}

(b) maximum x when $v = 0 \Rightarrow t = 3$

$\Rightarrow x = 27$ m

(c) maximum velocity when acceleration is zero

$\Rightarrow 24t - 12t^2 = 0 \Rightarrow t = 2 \Rightarrow v = 16$ m s^{-1}

However greatest speed when $t = 4$ $\therefore$ 64 m s^{-1}

17 (a) $v = 0 \Rightarrow t = -\frac{1}{2}$ or $1\frac{1}{2}$ (quadratic)

$\therefore P$ at $11.59\frac{1}{2}$ a.m, and Q at $12.01\frac{1}{2}$ p.m.

(b) $x = \frac{3}{8}t + \frac{1}{4}t^2 - \frac{1}{6}t^3 + \frac{5}{48}$ ($x = 0$ when $t = -\frac{1}{2}$)

(c) $t = 1\frac{1}{2} \Rightarrow x = \frac{2}{3} \Rightarrow$ average velocity $= \frac{2}{3} \div 2$

$= \frac{1}{3}$ km/min $= 20$ km/h

(d) Acceleration $= 0 \Rightarrow t = \frac{1}{2} \Rightarrow$ maximum

velocity $= \frac{1}{2}$ km/min = 30 km/h

18

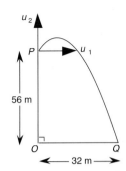

$\rightarrow : 32 = u_1 4 \Rightarrow u_1 = 8$ m s^{-1}

$\uparrow : -56 = u_2 4 - \frac{1}{2} \times 9.8 \times 16$

$\Rightarrow u_2 = 5.6$ m s^{-1}

$\therefore$

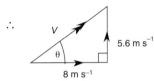

$\Rightarrow v = 9.77$ m s^{-1}

$\Rightarrow \theta = 35°$ to horizontal

19 $F = ma$ down the roof $\Rightarrow mg \sin 30° = ma$

$\Rightarrow a = 4.9$ m s^{-2}

Leaves roof with velocity v where

$v^2 = 0^2 + 2 \times 4.9 \times 5 \Rightarrow v = 7$ m s^{-1}

$\therefore$

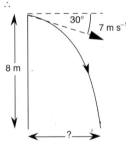

Resolve 7 m s^{-1} to get

6.06 m s^{-1}

$\therefore \downarrow : 8 = 3.5t + \frac{1}{2} \times 9.8 \times t^2 \Rightarrow t = 0.97$ seconds

(quadratic)

$\therefore \rightarrow :$ range = $6.06 \times 0.97 = 5.88$m

20 (a) $v_1 = \dfrac{t^2}{10}$ (no +c because starts from rest)

$\therefore t = 5 \Rightarrow v_1 = 2.5 \text{ m/s}$

(b) $v_2 = \dfrac{t^2}{10} - \dfrac{10}{t} + 2$

$\left(\displaystyle\int^{10} \dfrac{1}{t^2}\,dt = \int 10t^{-2}\,dt = -10t^{-1} = -\dfrac{10}{t}.\right.$

Also $v_2 = 5$ when $t = 5\Big)$

$\therefore t = 10 \Rightarrow v_2 = 11 \text{ m/s}$

21 (a) $a = 6t + 2 \;\therefore\; t = 2 \Rightarrow a = 14 \text{ m s}^{-2}$

(b) $x = t^3 + t^2 + c$

$\therefore t = 3, x = 36 + c$ and $t = 4, x = 80 + c$

$\Rightarrow$ distance covered = 44 m

22 (a) $a = k(7 - t^2)$

$\therefore \; v = k\left(7t - \dfrac{t^3}{3}\right) \; (t = 0 \text{ when } v \; 0)$

But $t = 3$ when $v = 6 \;\therefore\; k = \dfrac{1}{2}$

$\therefore \; v = \dfrac{1}{2}\left(7t - \dfrac{t^3}{3}\right)$

$\therefore \; s = \dfrac{1}{2}\left(\dfrac{7t^2}{2} - \dfrac{t^4}{12}\right) \; (t = 0 \text{ when } s = 0)$

$\therefore \; s = \dfrac{t^2}{24}\left(42 - t^2\right)$

(b) $v = 0 \Rightarrow t = \sqrt{21} \Rightarrow s = 18.375 \text{ m}.$

23 (a) $\downarrow : 3\dfrac{4}{15} = -49 \sin \alpha t + 4.9t^2$

$\rightarrow : 98 = 49 \cos \alpha t$

Eliminate t and get

$3\dfrac{4}{15} = -98 \tan \alpha + 19.6 \sec^2 \alpha$

$\therefore \; 3\dfrac{4}{15} = -98 \tan \alpha + 19.6\,(1 + \tan^2 \alpha)$

$\therefore \; 19.6 \tan^2 \alpha - 98 \tan \alpha + 16\dfrac{1}{3} = 0$

$\therefore \; 6 \tan^2 \alpha - 30 \tan \alpha + 5 = 0$

(b) Quadratic gives

$\tan \alpha = 4.83$ or $0.17 \Rightarrow \alpha = 78°$ or $10°$

(c) $\alpha = 78° \Rightarrow t = 10$ seconds and
$\alpha = 10° \Rightarrow t = 2$ seconds

$\therefore$ 2 seconds is smallest time.

Section 6

1 (a) A $\circlearrowright$: $6 \times 4 - 7 \times 4 = -4$ N m

(b) B $\circlearrowleft$: $6 \times 4 - 4 \times 4 = 8$ N m

(c) O $\circlearrowright$: $3 \times 2 - 7 \times 2 + 6 \times 2 - 4 \times 2 = -4$ N m

2 (a) A $\circlearrowleft$: $6 \times 2 - 8 \times 5 = -28$ N m

(b) B $\circlearrowright$: $-6 \times 3 = -18$ N m

3

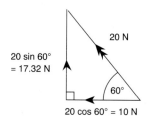

20 sin 60°
= 17.32 N

20 cos 60° = 10 N

A $\circlearrowleft$: $17.32 \times 10 = 173.2$ N m

4 (a) A $\circlearrowleft$: $9F \times a + 20F \sin 30° \times 3a = 39 \, Fa$

(b) C $\circlearrowright$: $6F \times 3a - 9F \times 2a = 0$

5 In all these questions there is a reaction, R, at the pivot. Therefore it's no good resolving vertically.

(a) pivot $\circlearrowright$: $6 \times 3 + F \times 3 = 4 \times 6 \;\therefore\; F = 2$ N

(b) pivot $\circlearrowright$: $F \times 6 = 7 \times 2 + 5 \times 3 \;\therefore\; F = 4\dfrac{5}{6}$ N

(c) pivot $\circlearrowright$: $8 \times 6 + F \times 4 = 20 \times 4 \;\therefore\; F = 8$ N

(d) pivot $\circlearrowright$: $8 \times 3 = 5 \times 1 + 3 \times 1 + F \times 4$
$\therefore F = 4$ N

6

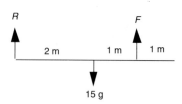

R is force at hinge and F is the supporting force. Once again, it is no good resolving vertically because that gives

$R + F = 15$ g.

$\therefore$ hinge $\circlearrowright$: 15 g $\times 2 = F \times 3$

$\therefore F = 10$ g or 98 N

$\therefore$ hinge $\circlearrowright$: $15g \times 4 + 15g \times 4 = F \times 3$

$\therefore F = 30g$ or 294 N

7

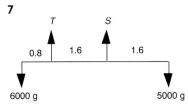

$\uparrow : T + S = 11\,000$ g

and $\circlearrowright$: $T \times 0.8 + S \times 2.4 = 5000$ g $\times 4$

$\therefore S = 68.6$ kN

$\therefore T = 39.2$ kN

8

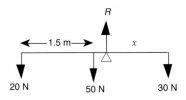

$\uparrow : R = 100$ N

$\circlearrowright$: end : $Rx = 50 \times 1.5 + 20 \times 3$

$\therefore x = 1.35$ m

9 (a) $\uparrow : X + Y = 40$

end $\circlearrowright$: $0.2X + 0.9Y = 30 \times 0.6$

$\therefore X = 25\frac{5}{7}$ N, $Y = 14\frac{2}{7}$ N

(b)

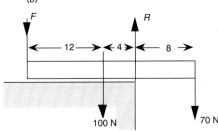

edge $\circlearrowleft$: $70 \times 8 = 100 \times 4 + F \times 16$

$\therefore F = 10$ N

(c) $\uparrow : 5 \sin 30° + 5 = X \quad \therefore X = 7.5$ N

$\rightarrow : Y = 5 \cos 30° \quad \therefore Y = 4.33$ N

I didn't need to use moments this time.

10 $\uparrow : Y = 4$

$\rightarrow : X + 3 = 5 \therefore X = 2$

corner $\circlearrowright$: $5a + Y(a + d) = 0 \therefore d = -2\frac{1}{4}a$

11

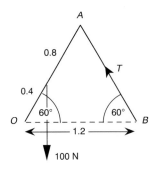

There are forces acting at the hinge O
$\therefore$ we take moments about O.

$O \circlearrowright$: $100 \times 0.4 \cos 60° = T \sin 60° \times 1.2$
$\therefore T = 19.2$ N

12 There are forces acting at B $\therefore$ we take moments about B. Let force required be F.

$\therefore B \circlearrowright$: $200 \times 1.2 = F \times 0.2 \cos 30°$
$\therefore F = 1386$ N

13 $A \circlearrowright$: $Wa = T \sin 30° \times 2a \therefore T = W$

14

$\uparrow : X + Z = 5 \qquad \therefore X = \frac{1}{2}$

$\rightarrow : Y = 4 \qquad Y = 4$

end $\circlearrowright$: $5a + Ya = Z2a \qquad Z = 4\frac{1}{2}$

15

				Total
Mass (kg)	1	4	8	13
Distance from A	2	9	5	x

$\therefore 1 \times 2 + 4 \times 9 + 8 \times 5 = 13\bar{x} \therefore \bar{x} = 6$ m

16

				Total
Mass (kg)	4	1	5	10
Distance from A	0	24	40	$\bar{x}$

$\therefore 4 \times 0 + 1 \times 24 + 5 \times 40 = 10\bar{x} \therefore \bar{x} = 22.4$ cm

17 $5 \times -4 + 3 \times 1 + 2 \times 3 = 10\bar{x}$ $\therefore$ $\bar{x} = -1.1$

18 $\pi \times 5^2 \times 0 + 2 \times \pi \times 5 \times 9 \times 4.5 = 115\pi\bar{y}$

    $\therefore$ $\bar{y} = 3.52$ cm (2 d.p.)

19 $80 \times 5 + 24 \times 12 = 104 \times \bar{y}$

    $\therefore$ $\bar{y} = 6.62$ cm (2 d.p.)

20 $144 \times 9 - 16\pi \times 14 = (144 - 16\pi)\bar{y}$

    $\therefore$ $\bar{y} = 6.32$ cm (2 d.p.)

21   (a) $8000 \times 10 + 1000 \times 25 = 9000\bar{y}$

    $\therefore$ $\bar{y} = 11.67$ mm (2 d.p.)

    (In this case, use *volumes* to represent the mass.)

    (b) $16\pi \times 0.5 + 9\pi \times 1.5 + 4\pi \times 2.5 + \pi \times 3.5$
                                       $= 30\pi \times \bar{y}$

    $\therefore$ $\bar{y} = 1\frac{1}{6}$ cm above the base

22

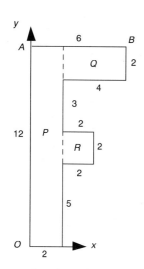

Separate into shapes P, Q and R as shown

	$R +$	$Q +$	$R =$	F–shape
Area	24	8	4	36
x-coordinate	1	4	3	$\bar{x}$
y-coordinate	6	11	6	$\bar{y}$

$\therefore$ $24 \times 1 + 8 \times 4 + 4 \times 3 = 36\bar{x}$ $\therefore$ $\bar{x} = 1\frac{8}{9}$ cm

$\therefore$ $24 \times 6 + 8 \times 11 + 4 \times 6 = 36\bar{y}$ $\therefore$ $\bar{y} = 7\frac{1}{9}$ cm

23

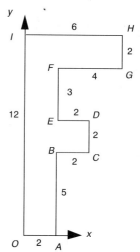

$OA + AB + BC + CD + DE + EF + FG + GH + HI$
$+ IO =$ Whole thing.

These are set out in the table below.

Length	2	5	2	2	2	3	4	2	6	12	40
x-coord	1	2	3	4	3	2	4	6	3	0	$\bar{x}$
y-coord	0	2.5	5	6	7	8.5	10	11	12	6	$\bar{y}$

    $\therefore$ $\bar{x} = 2\frac{1}{10}$, $\bar{y} = 7$

24

	Rectangle	centre hole	end hole	= wanted shape
Area	4000	100π	100π	$4000 - 200\pi$
x-coordinate	50	50	90	$\bar{x}$
y-coordinate	20	20	20	$\bar{y}$

$\therefore$ $4000 \times 50 - 100\pi \times 50 - 100\pi \times 90 =$
                              $(4000 - 200\pi)\bar{x}$

$\therefore$ $\bar{x} = 46.27$ (2 d.p.), $\bar{y} = 20$

25

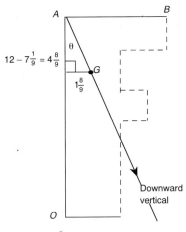

$$\Rightarrow \tan\theta = \frac{1\frac{8}{9}}{4\frac{8}{9}} \Rightarrow \theta = 21.1°\ (1\ \text{d.p.})$$

26

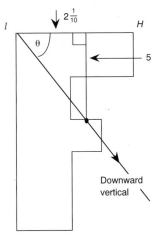

$$\Rightarrow \tan\theta = \frac{5}{2\frac{1}{10}} \Rightarrow \theta = 67.2°\ (1\ \text{d.p.})$$

27

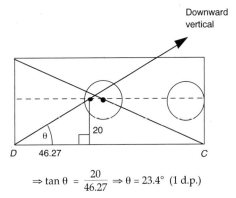

$$\Rightarrow \tan\theta = \frac{20}{46.27} \Rightarrow \theta = 23.4°\ (1\ \text{d.p.})$$

28   (a)

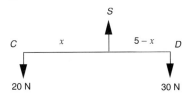

$\uparrow : S = 50\ \text{N}$

$C\,\curvearrowright : Sx = 30 \times 5 \qquad \therefore\ CQ = x = 3\ \text{m}$

(b) $S = 50\ \text{N}$

(c)

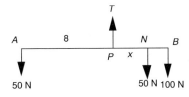

$\uparrow : T = 200\ \text{N}$

$P\,\curvearrowright : 50 \times 8 = 50x + 100 \times 3$

$\therefore\ PN = x = 2\ \text{m}$

(d) $T = 200\ \text{N}$

29 (a)

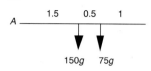

$A \measuredangle : 150g \times 1.5 + 75g \times 2 = 375g$

∴ 3675 N m

(b) $A \measuredangle : 150g \times 1.5 + 75g \times 3 = 450g$

∴ 4410 N m

30 ∴ $3 \times 1 + 5 \times -1 + 2 \times 2 + 4 \times -1 = 14\bar{x}$

∴ $\bar{x} = -\frac{1}{7}$

∴ $3 \times 6 + 5 \times 5 + 2 \times -3 + 4 \times -4 = 14\bar{y}$

∴ $\bar{y} = 1\frac{1}{2}$

31 Take X as the origin and XY extended as the x-axis. The x-coordinate of the shaded area's centre of gravity is $-\frac{4}{9}r$.

Big circle – Small circle = Shaded area

Area	πR^2	πr^2	$\pi(R^2 - r^2)$
x-coordinate	0	$R - r$	$-\frac{4}{9}r$

∴ $\pi R^2 \times 0 - \pi r^2 (R - r) = \pi(R^2 - r^2) \times -\frac{4}{9}r$

∴ $r = (R + r)\frac{4}{9}$

∴ $9r = 4R + 4r \Rightarrow R = \frac{5}{4}r$

32 (a) 2 cm

(b) $16 \times 2 - 4 \times 3 = 12 d \Rightarrow d = 1\frac{2}{3}$ cm

(c) $\tan \theta = \dfrac{1\frac{2}{3}}{2} \Rightarrow \theta = 40°$

Section 7

1 $3 \times 21 - 3 \times 6 = 8t \Rightarrow t = 5.625$ seconds

2 $0.12 \times 20 = F \times 0.1 \Rightarrow F = 24$ N

3 $v^2 = 0^2 + 2 \times 9.8 \times 1.25 \Rightarrow v = 4.95$ m s^{-1} (2d.p.)

$\Rightarrow$ Impulse $= 0.09 \times 4.95 = 0.45$ N s

4 The impulse is away from the bat and so all speeds must have that direction

∴ $u = -6$ m s^{-1}, $v = 12$ m s^{-1}, $m = 0.16$

∴ $0.16 \times 12 - 0.16 \times -6 =$ impulse

$\Rightarrow$ impulse $= 2.88$ N s

5 $0.005u = 0.01$ ∴ $u = 2$ m s^{-1} (initial velocity)

$\Rightarrow 0^2 = 2^2 + 2 \times a \times 0.5$

∴ $a = -4$ m s^{-2} (acceleration)

but normal reaction = weight = 0.049 N

∴ frictional force $= \mu \times 0.049 = 0.005 \times 4$ (*ma*)

$\Rightarrow \mu = 0.41$ (2d.p.)

6 $4 \times 10 = F \times 1 \Rightarrow F = 40$ N

7 (a) $5 \times 14 = 7u \Rightarrow u = 10$ m s^{-1}

(b) $2 \times 10 - 2 \times 0 =$ impulse

$\Rightarrow$ impulse $= 20$ N s

8 (a) $4 \times 5 + 2 \times 2 = 6u \Rightarrow u = 4$ m s^{-1}

(b) $2 \times 4 - 2 \times 2 =$ impulse $\Rightarrow$ impulse $= 4$ N s

9 (a) $5 \times 6 - 2 \times 8 = 7u \Rightarrow u = 2$ m s^{-1}

(b) $5 \times 2 - 5 \times 6 =$ impulse

$\Rightarrow$ impulse $= -20$ N s

(c) 20 N s

10 $a = 4$ m s^{-2}

(a) $v = 0 + 4 \times 8 = 32$ m s^{-1}

(b) $s = \left(\dfrac{0 + 32}{2}\right)8 = 128$ m

(c) $10 \times 32 + 6 \times 0 = 16u \Rightarrow u = 20$ m s^{-1}

11 (a) $30 \times 12 = 40u \Rightarrow u = 9$ m s^{-1}

(b) $a = 0.5$ m s^{-2}

$s = 9 \times 10 + \frac{1}{2} \times 0.5 \times 10^2 = 115$ m

12 $m \times 550 = (0.49 + m) \times 11 \Rightarrow m = 0.01$ kg

13 $20 \times 400 = 12 \times 700 + 8u \Rightarrow u = -50$ m s^{-1}

∴ velocity of 50 m s^{-1} in the opposite direction.

14 $v^2 = 0^2 + 2 \times 9.8 \times 2.5 \Rightarrow v = 7 \text{ m s}^{-1}$ before impact.

After impact let the 7 kg system be moving with velocity u.

$\therefore \ 1 \times 7 = 7u \ \therefore \ u = 1 \text{ m s}^{-1}$

15 (a)

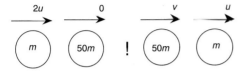

$\therefore \ m \times 2u + 50m \times 0 = 50m \times v + m \times u$

$\therefore \ 2mu = 50mv + mu \qquad \therefore \ v = \dfrac{u}{50}$

(b)

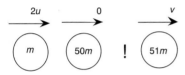

$\therefore \ m \times 2u + 50m \times 0 = 51mv \quad \therefore \ v = \dfrac{2u}{51}$

16 Let V be the common speed after impact.

$\therefore \ mv = (m + M)V \Rightarrow V = mv / (m + M).$

17 Gain in K.E. $= \dfrac{1}{2} \times 8 \times 6^2 - \dfrac{1}{2} \times 8 \times 4^2 = 80 \text{ J}$

18 (a) $225 \times 4 + 75 \times 0 = 300u \Rightarrow u = 3 \text{ m s}^{-1}$

(b) KE before $= \dfrac{1}{2} \times 225 \times 4^2 = 1800 \text{ J}$

K.E. after $= \dfrac{1}{2} \times 300 \times 3^2 = 1350 \text{ J}$

$\therefore \ $ Loss of KE $= 450 \text{ J}$

19 (a) $500 = 100a \Rightarrow a = 5 \text{ m s}^{-2}$

(b) $v^2 = 2 \times 5 \times 40 \Rightarrow v = 20 \text{ m s}^{-1}$

(c) $100 \times 20 - 10 \times 35 = 110u$

$\Rightarrow u = 15 \text{ m s}^{-1}$

(d) $196 = 100a \Rightarrow a = -1.96 \text{ m s}^{-2}$
(so his retardation is 1.96 m s^{-2})

(e) $v^2 = 15^2 - 2 \times 1.96 \times 36.73 \Rightarrow v = 9 \text{ m s}^{-1}$

(f) $\downarrow : 78.4 = 4.9t^2 \Rightarrow t = 4$ seconds

(g) $\rightarrow : s = 9 \times 4 = 36 \text{ m}$

(h)

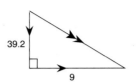

$\therefore \ 40.2 \text{ m s}^{-1}$ at $77°$ to horizontal

(1 d.p. and 2 s.f. respectively)

(i) K.E. before $= \dfrac{1}{2} \times 100 \times 20^2 + \dfrac{1}{2} \times 10 \times 35^2$

$= 26\,125 \text{ J}$

K.E. after $= \dfrac{1}{2} \times 110 \times 40.2^2 = 88\,882 \text{ J}$

$\therefore \ $ gain in kinetic energy $= 62\,757 \text{ J}$

(The reason that *K.E. is gained* in this example is that *work is being done*. We shall return to this in Section 9.)

Incidentally, you will be pleased to know that the cyclist was also a strong swimmer and successfully swam ashore.

20 (a) Let $u = 21\,\lambda$ and $v = 26\,\lambda$

$\therefore \ 0.08 \times 1.5 + 0.12 \times 1 = 0.08 \times 21\,\lambda + 0.12 \times 26\,\lambda$

$\therefore \ \lambda = 0.05$

$\therefore \ u = 21\,\lambda = 1.05$ and $v = 26\,\lambda = 1.3$

(b) $0.08 \times 1.05 - 0.08 \times 1.5 = $ Impulse

$\therefore \ $ Impulse $= (-)\,0.036 \text{ N s}.$

Section 8

1

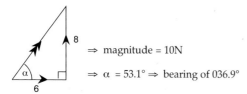

$\Rightarrow$ magnitude = 10N

$\Rightarrow \alpha = 53.1° \Rightarrow$ bearing of 036.9°

2 $\mathbf{a} = 2\mathbf{i} + 3\mathbf{j} \Rightarrow$ magnitude = 3.6 m s^{-2} (1d.p.)

3 $a - 8 = 0 \Rightarrow a = 8$

4 $b + 10 = 0 \Rightarrow b = -10$

5 $a + 4 = 2a - 6 \Rightarrow a = 10$

6 $5\mathbf{i} + 12\mathbf{j} = 5\mathbf{a} \Rightarrow \mathbf{a} = (\mathbf{i} + 2.4\mathbf{j})$ m s^{-2}

7 $10 + p = 4 \times 8, 4 + q = 4 \times 12 \Rightarrow p = 22, q = 44$

8 (a) $5\mathbf{i} + 8\mathbf{j} = 10\mathbf{a} \Rightarrow \mathbf{a} = (0.5\mathbf{i} + 0.8\mathbf{j})$ m s^{-2}

(b) $-5\mathbf{i}$ N   (c) $-8\mathbf{j}$ N

9 $4\mathbf{i} + 3\mathbf{j}$ has magnitude 5

$\therefore 2(4\mathbf{i} + 3\mathbf{j}) = (8\mathbf{i} + 6\mathbf{j})$ m s^{-2}

10 $-5\mathbf{i} + 12\mathbf{j}$ has magnitude 13

$\therefore 0.5(-5\mathbf{i} + 12\mathbf{j}) = (-2.5\mathbf{i} + 6\mathbf{j})$ m s^{-1}

11 $4(3\mathbf{i} - 4\mathbf{j}) = (12\mathbf{i} - 16\mathbf{j})$ N s

12 $7\mathbf{i} + 24\mathbf{j}$ has magnitude 25

$\therefore 0.5(7\mathbf{i} + 24\mathbf{j}) = (3.5\mathbf{i} + 12\mathbf{j})$ N

13 (a) $10 + b = 3 \times 3, 2 + a = 3 \times 4 \Rightarrow b = -1, a = 10$

(b) $\rightarrow : 20 = U_x + 3 \times 3 \Rightarrow U_x = -11$

$\uparrow : 20 = U_y + 4 \times 3 \Rightarrow U_y = 8$

$\Rightarrow$ initial velocity = $(-11\mathbf{i} + 8\mathbf{j})$

14 $a = 5\mathbf{i} - 2\mathbf{j} \quad \Rightarrow \mathbf{v} = (5t + 4)\mathbf{i} + (-2t + 10)\mathbf{j}$

$\Rightarrow \mathbf{r} = \left(\dfrac{5t^2}{2} + 4t + 1\right)\mathbf{i} + (-t^2 + 10t + 1)\mathbf{j}$

Now $-t^2 + 10t + 1$ is greatest when the derivative = 0

$\therefore -2t + 10 = 0 \Rightarrow t = 5$

$\Rightarrow$ maximum $y = -25 + 50 + 1 = 26$

15 (a) K.E. $= \frac{1}{2} \times 4 \times (3^2 + 4^2) = 50$J

(b) Momentum $= 4(3\mathbf{i} + 4\mathbf{j}) = 12\mathbf{i} + 16\mathbf{j}$ N s

16 (a) $2(1.5\mathbf{i} + 8\mathbf{j}) + 5(-2\mathbf{i} + 8\mathbf{j}) = 7\mathbf{V}$

$\Rightarrow \mathbf{V} = (-\mathbf{i} + 8\mathbf{j})$ m s^{-1}

(b) Loss of K.E. $= -\frac{1}{2} \times 7 \times (1^2 + 8^2) +$

$\left\{\frac{1}{2} \times 2 \times (1.5^2 + 8^2) + \frac{1}{2} \times 5(-2^2 + 8^2)\right\}$

$= -227.5 + 236.25 = 8.75$ J

(c) $2(-\mathbf{i} + 8\mathbf{j}) - 2(1.5\mathbf{i} + 8\mathbf{j}) = -5\mathbf{i}$ N s

17 (a) Momentum after =
$50(250\mathbf{i} + 50\mathbf{j}) + 40(100\mathbf{i} + 200\mathbf{j})$

$= 16\,500\mathbf{i} + 10\,500\mathbf{j}$.

This is different from the momentum before of $90(200\mathbf{i} + 100\mathbf{j})$

$\therefore$ It cannot be an internal explosion.

(b) $90(200\mathbf{i} + 100\mathbf{j}) + 15V = 16500\mathbf{i} + 10500\mathbf{j}$

$\Rightarrow V = (-100\mathbf{i} + 100\mathbf{j})$m s^{-1}

18 $\dot{\mathbf{r}} = 6t\mathbf{i} + 4\mathbf{j} \therefore t = 4 \Rightarrow \dot{\mathbf{r}} = (24\mathbf{i} + 4\mathbf{j})$ m s^{-1}

$\ddot{\mathbf{r}} = 6\mathbf{i}$ for all t

19 $\mathbf{a} = 2\mathbf{i} - \mathbf{j}, \mathbf{v} = 2t\mathbf{i} - t\mathbf{j}, \mathbf{r} = (t^2 + 3)\mathbf{i} + (-\dfrac{t^2}{2} + 1)\mathbf{j}$

20 $\mathbf{a} = 6t\mathbf{i} + \mathbf{j} \therefore t = 3 \Rightarrow \mathbf{a} = (18\mathbf{i} + \mathbf{j})$ m s^{-2}

$\mathbf{r} = t^3\mathbf{i} + \left(\dfrac{t^2}{2} - t\right)\mathbf{j} \therefore t = 3 \Rightarrow \mathbf{r} = (27\mathbf{i} + 1.5\mathbf{j})$ m

21 $\dot{\mathbf{r}} = 6t\mathbf{i} + 5\mathbf{j}, \mathbf{r} = 6\mathbf{i} \Rightarrow$ acceleration constant.

$\therefore F = 6mi$ N

22 $\mathbf{a} = \mathbf{i} - 3\mathbf{j}, \mathbf{v} = (t + 1)\mathbf{i} + (-3t - 1)\mathbf{j}$

$\Rightarrow \mathbf{r} = \left(\dfrac{t^2}{2} + t + 1\right)\mathbf{i} + \left(-\dfrac{3t^2}{2} - t + 1\right)\mathbf{j}$

23 $m\mathbf{a} = 3\mathbf{i} + 3t\mathbf{j} \Rightarrow m\mathbf{v} = 3t\mathbf{i} + \dfrac{3t^2}{2}\mathbf{j}$

$\therefore t = 5 \Rightarrow$ momentum $= (15\mathbf{i} + 37.5\mathbf{j})$ N s

24 $t = 0, \mathbf{r} = -3\mathbf{i} + 12\mathbf{j} ; t = 1, \mathbf{r} = 8\mathbf{j}$

$t = 2, \mathbf{r} = 3\mathbf{i} + 4\mathbf{j} ; t = 3, \mathbf{r} = 6\mathbf{i}$

$t = 4, \mathbf{r} = 9\mathbf{i} - 4\mathbf{j}$.

(a) The path is shown in the following diagram.

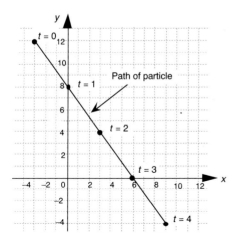

$t = 0$

Path of particle

$t = 1$

$t = 2$

$t = 3$

$t = 4$

(b) The particle is closest to the origin when the magnitude of:

$\mathbf{r} = (3t - 3)\mathbf{i} + (12 - 4t)\mathbf{j}$ is least.

This is equivalent to finding the minimum value of:

$(3t - 3)^2 + (12 - 4t)^2$

Simplify the brackets to get $25t^2 - 114t + 153$

Now differentiate and put equal to zero

$\therefore \; 50t - 114 = 0 \Rightarrow t = 2.28$

(c) Looking at the diagram, this certainly seems reasonable – the particle is closest somewhere between $t = 2$ and $t = 3$.

Finally $t = 2.28 \Rightarrow \mathbf{r} = 3.84\mathbf{i} + 2.88\mathbf{i}$

The magnitude of $\mathbf{r} = \sqrt{3.84^2 + 2.88^2} = 4.8$ cm

(Alternatively you could drop a perpendicular from the origin to the line $3y + 4x = 24$, solve simultaneously and get $x = 3.84$, $y = 2.88$. Then substitute back and get $t = 2.28$)

An important example: give it some thought.

25 $(5\mathbf{i} + 4\mathbf{j})$ m s^{-1}

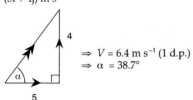

4

5

α

$\Rightarrow V = 6.4$ m s^{-1} (1 d.p.)
$\Rightarrow \alpha = 38.7°$

$\therefore$ 6.4 m s^{-1} on a bearing of 051.3° (1 d.p.)

26 $3\mathbf{i} - (\mathbf{i} + 6\mathbf{j}) = (2\mathbf{i} - 6\mathbf{j})$ m s^{-1}

27 (a) $(t - 2)\mathbf{i} + (3t - 1)\mathbf{j}$

(b) $(t - 2)^2 + (3t - 1)^2 = 10t^2 - 10t + 5$

Differentiate and get zero

$\therefore \; 20t - 10 = 0 \Rightarrow t = 0.5$

(c) $t = 0.5$ in (a) gives $-1.5\mathbf{i} + 0.5\mathbf{j} \Rightarrow$

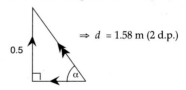

0.5

α

$\Rightarrow d = 1.58$ m (2 d.p.)

28 (a) $\dot{\mathbf{r}} = (2t - 4)\mathbf{i} + (3t^2 + 2ft)\mathbf{j}$

(b) $\dot{\mathbf{r}} = 0 \qquad \Rightarrow 2t - 4 = 0$ and $3t^2 + 2ft = 0$
$\Rightarrow t = 2 \; \therefore \; f = -3$

29 After the collison both particles must have direction $16\mathbf{i} - 12\mathbf{j}$.

But $16\mathbf{i} - 12\mathbf{j} \Rightarrow$

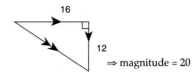

16

12

$\Rightarrow$ magnitude = 20

$\therefore$ a **unit vector** in the direction of motion will be $\frac{1}{20}(16\mathbf{i} - 12\mathbf{j}) = 0.8\mathbf{i} - 0.6\mathbf{j}$.

(A **unit** vector is a vector whose magnitude is one.)

(a) $0.8\mathbf{i} - 0.6\mathbf{j}$

(b) $0.2(16\mathbf{i} - 12\mathbf{j}) = 0.2\mathbf{V} + 10(0.8\mathbf{i} - 0.6\mathbf{j})$, where $\mathbf{V}$ is velocity vector of A after collision (the conservation of momentum equation).

$\therefore \; \mathbf{V} = (-24\mathbf{i} + 18\mathbf{j})$ m s^{-1}, velocity of A

and $(8\mathbf{i} - 6\mathbf{j})$ m s^{-1}, velocity of B

(c) Impulse $= 0.2(-24\mathbf{i} + 18\mathbf{j}) - 0.2(16\mathbf{i} - 12\mathbf{j})$
$= (-8\mathbf{i} + 6\mathbf{j})$ N s

30 (a) $\dot{\mathbf{r}} = (2 - 6t)\mathbf{i} + 4t\,\mathbf{j}$

$\therefore \; t = 2 \Rightarrow \dot{\mathbf{r}} = -10\mathbf{i} + 8\mathbf{j}$

(b) $\sqrt{-10^2 + 8} = \sqrt{164}$ m s^{-1}

31 (a) At time t: position vector of $Q = 2\sqrt{3}\mathbf{i} + \mathbf{v}t$

and position vector of $P = 2\mathbf{j} + 3\mathbf{j}t$

They collide at time T

$\therefore \; 2\sqrt{3}\mathbf{i} + \mathbf{v}T = 2\mathbf{j} + 3Tj$

$\therefore \; T(\mathbf{v} - 3\mathbf{j}) = 2\mathbf{j} - 2\sqrt{3}\mathbf{i}$

But the velocity of Q relative to P is $\mathbf{v} - 3\mathbf{j}$

which equals $\frac{1}{T}(2\mathbf{j} - 2\sqrt{3}\mathbf{i})$

$\therefore \; \mathbf{v} - 3\mathbf{j}$ has the direction $2\mathbf{j} - 2\sqrt{3}\mathbf{i}$

(b) $\mathbf{v} - 3\mathbf{j} = \frac{1}{T}(2\mathbf{j} - 2\sqrt{3}\mathbf{i})$

$\Rightarrow \mathbf{v} = -\frac{2}{T}\sqrt{3}\mathbf{i} + \left(\frac{2}{T} + 3\right)\mathbf{j}$ $\therefore k = \frac{2}{T}$

(c) $\mathbf{v} = -k\sqrt{3}\mathbf{i} + (k+3)\mathbf{j}$ has magnitude $3\sqrt{3}$

$\therefore$ $3k^2 + (k+3)^2 = 27$ $\therefore k = 1.5$ or -3
(quadratic)

But $k > 0$ $\therefore k = 1.5$

(d) $T = \frac{2}{k} = 1\frac{1}{3}$

Section 9

1 $\frac{1}{2} \times 1000 \times 8^2 = 32\,000$ J or 32 kJ

2 $50 \times 1.65 \times 8 = 660$ J

3 $(40 \times 9.8 \times \sin 60° - 60) \times 10 = \frac{1}{2} \times 40 \times v^2$

$\Rightarrow v = 11.82$ m s^{-1} (2d.p.)

4 $R \times 2.4 = \frac{1}{2} \times 0.01 \times 600^2$ $\Rightarrow R = 750$ N

5 Component of the weight down the plane = $20 \times 9.8 \times \sin 30°$.

$\therefore$ $20 \times 9.8 \times \sin 30° \times 5 = \frac{1}{2} \times 20 \times v^2$

$\Rightarrow v = 7$ m s^{-1}

6 Take zero P.E. at the level of the hole H.

$\therefore$ $\frac{1}{2} \times 0.02 \times 3^2 + 0.02 \times 9.8 \times 6 = \frac{1}{2} \times 0.02 \times v^2$

$\Rightarrow v = 11.3$ m s^{-1} (1d.p.)

(Using conservation of energy.)

7 (a) Taking the initial level as zero P.E., the car originally has no total energy. When it reaches B its P.E. is again zero and so it can't have any K.E. there either.

$\therefore$ Car comes to instantaneous rest at B then car does the return journey, just getting back to A. The car continues to oscillate from A to B.

(b) The original energy of the car is now $\frac{1}{2} \times 1000 \times 6^2 = 18$ kJ.

If it reaches C its potential energy there will be $1000 \times 9.8 \times 10 = 98$ kJ. But the car cannot gain energy and so it cannot reach C.

$\therefore$ Somewhere between B and C the car comes to instantaneous rest. Then the car does the return journey, reappearing at A with a velocity of 6 m s^{-1}.

(c) The original energy of the car is now

$\frac{1}{2} \times 1000 \times 15^2 = 112.5$ kJ.

At C its potential energy would be

$1000 \times 9.8 \times 10 = 98$ kJ

$\therefore$ Its kinetic energy at C will be

112.5 kJ – 98 kJ = 14.5 kJ

$\therefore$ $14\,500 = \frac{1}{2} \times 1000 \times u^2$ $\Rightarrow u = 5.4$ m s^{-1} (1d.p.)

$\therefore$ Car goes over the peak at C with a velocity of 5.4 m s^{-1}. So far so good!

Using conservation of energy at D we get

$\frac{1}{2} \times 1000 \times v^2 - 1000 \times 9.8 \times 5 = 112\,500$

$\Rightarrow v = 18$ m s^{-1} (2 s.f.)

$\therefore$ Car flies off horizontally at D with a velocity of 18 m s^{-1}

$\therefore \rightarrow : 9 = 18t \Rightarrow t = 0.5$

$\therefore$ Car takes 0.5 seconds to cross the gap.

$\therefore \downarrow : s = \frac{1}{2} \times 9.8 \times 0.5^2 \Rightarrow s = 1.225$

$\therefore$ Car drops a vertical distance of 1.225 m in that time. But the actual gap downwards from D to E is 0.5 m.

$\therefore$ The car misses the rail at E and …!

8 $5000 \times 9.8 \times 0.4 = 19.6$ kW

9   3 birds a minute $\Rightarrow$ 0.05 birds a second.

$\therefore$ $0.05 \times 0.08 \times 9.8 \times 20 = 0.784$ W

$\therefore$ Necessary power $\quad= 2 \times 0.784$
$\qquad\qquad\qquad\qquad = 1.57$ W (2 d.p.)

10   120 kg a minute $\Rightarrow$ 2 kg a second.

$10^2 = 2 \times a \times 4 \Rightarrow$ acceleration $= 12.5$ m s^{-2}

Let F be driving force of the fire pump

$\therefore$ $F - 2 \times 9.8 = 2 \times 12.5 \Rightarrow F = 44.6$ N

$\therefore$ Work done by fire pump $= 44.6 \times 4 = 178.4$ J

$\therefore$ Power $= 178.4$ J per second $= 178.4$ W

11   Force down plane $= 800 \times 9.8 \times \frac{1}{10} + 200 = 984$ N

$\therefore$ Power $= 984 \times 20 = 19\,680$ W

12   Inclination of $\sin \theta \left(\frac{1}{14}\right) \Rightarrow$

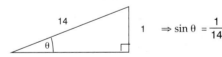

$\Rightarrow \sin \theta = \frac{1}{14}$

Going up the plane: total force downwards

$\qquad = 200 \times 9.8 \times \frac{1}{14} + k10^2 = 140 + 100k$

Coming down the plane: total force downwards

$\qquad = 200 \times 9.8 \times \frac{1}{14} - k20^2 = 140 - 400k$

But power developed is the same.

$\therefore$ $(140 + 100k)10 = (140 - 400k)20$

$\Rightarrow k = \frac{7}{45}$

$\Rightarrow$ Power $= \left(140 + 100 \times \frac{7}{45}\right)10 = 1.6$ kW (1 d.p.)

13   (a)

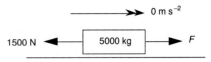

$\therefore$ $F = 1500$ N $\therefore$ Power $= 40\,000 = 1500 \times v$

$\Rightarrow v = 26\frac{2}{3}$ m s^{-1} (or 96 kmh^{-1})

(b)

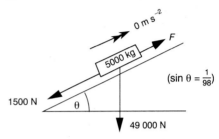

$\therefore$ $F = 1500 + 49\,000 \times \frac{1}{98} = 2000$ N

$\therefore$ Power $= 40\,000 = 2000 \times v$

$\Rightarrow v = 20$ m s^{-1} (or 72 km h^{-1})

14

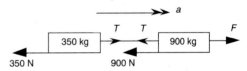

54 kmh$^{-1} = 15$ m s^{-1}

$\therefore$ Power $= 45\,000 = F \times 15 \Rightarrow F = 3000$ N

Also $F - 900 - 350 = 1250a \Rightarrow F - 1250 = 1250a$

$\Rightarrow a = 1.4$ m s^{-2}

and $T - 350 = 350a$

$\Rightarrow T = 840$ N

15

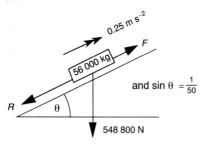

$$\text{Power} = 240\,000 = F \times 5 \implies F = 48\,000 \text{ N}$$

$$\therefore\ 48\,000 - R - 548\,800 \times \frac{1}{50} = 56\,000 \times 0.25$$

$$\implies R = 23\,024 \text{ N}$$

16 (a)

$$\text{Power} = 400 = F \times 5 \implies F = 80 \text{ N} \implies R = 80 \text{ N}$$

(b)

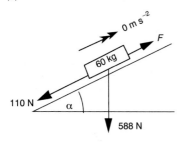

$$\therefore\ F = 110 + 588 \times \frac{1}{12} = 159 \text{ N}$$

$$\therefore\ \text{Power} = 400 = 159 \times v$$

$$\implies V = 2.52 \text{ m/s}\ (2 \text{ d.p.})$$

(c) $\text{Power} = 400 = F \times 2 \implies F = 200 \text{ N}$

$$\therefore\ 200 = 110 + 588 \sin \alpha \implies \alpha = 8.8° \ (1 \text{ d.p.})$$

17

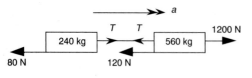

$$\therefore\ 1200 - T - 120 = 560a$$

$$\text{and } T - 80 = 240\,a$$

$$\implies \text{(a)}\ \ a = 1.25 \text{ m s}^{-1}$$

$$\implies \text{(b)}\ \ T = 380 \text{ N}$$

(c) $\therefore\ \text{Power} = 1200 \times 12 = 14\,400 \text{ J}$

(d) For the uphill journey:

$$1200 - 120 - 560 \times 9.8 \times \frac{1}{16} - T = 560a$$

$$\text{and } T - 80 - 240 \times 9.8 \times \frac{1}{16} = 240a$$

$$\therefore\ a = 0.6375 \text{ m s}^{-2}$$

(e) $\therefore\ T = 380 \text{ N again}$

18 (a)

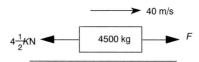

$$39\,600 = F \times 40 \quad \therefore F = 990 \text{ N}$$

But zero acceleration

$$\therefore\ F = 4\frac{1}{2}K \quad \therefore\ K = 220$$

(b)

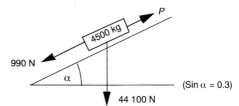

Zero acceleration

$$\therefore\quad P = 990 + 44\,100 \times 0.3$$

$$\therefore\quad P = 14\,220 \text{ N}$$

Same power $\therefore\ 39\,600 = 14\,220\,v$

$$\therefore\ v = 2.78 \text{ m s}^{-1}\ (2 \text{ d.p.})$$

$$\therefore\ \text{K.E.} = \frac{1}{2} \times 4500 \times 2.78^2 = 17000 \text{ J}\ (2 \text{ s.f.})$$